Stories by Foreign Authors: Russian

Various

Contents

STORIES BY FOREIGN AUTHORS: RUSSIAN

BY

Various

MUMU
BY
IVAN TURGENEV

From "Torrents of Spring." Translated by Constance Garnett.

In one of the outlying streets of Moscow, in a gray house with white columns and a balcony, warped all askew, there was once living a lady, a widow, surrounded by a numerous household of serfs. Her sons were in the government service at Petersburg; her daughters were married; she went out very little, and in solitude lived through the last years of her miserly and dreary old age. Her day, a joyless and gloomy day, had long been over; but the evening of her life was blacker than night.

Of all her servants, the most remarkable personage was the porter, Gerasim, a man full twelve inches over the normal height, of heroic build, and deaf and dumb from his birth. The lady, his owner, had brought him up from the village where he lived alone in a little hut, apart from his brothers, and was reckoned about the most punctual of her peasants in the payment of the seignorial dues. Endowed with extraordinary strength, he did the work of four men; work flew apace under his hands, and it was a pleasant sight to see him when he was ploughing, while, with his huge palms pressing hard upon the plough, he seemed alone, unaided by his poor horse, to cleave the yielding bosom of the earth, or when, about St. Peter's Day, he plied his scythe with a furious energy that might have mown a young birch copse up by the roots, or swiftly and untiringly wielded a flail over two yards long; while the hard oblong muscles of his shoulders rose and fell like a lever. His perpetual silence lent a solemn dignity to his unwearying labor. He was a splendid peasant, and, except for his affliction, any girl would have been glad to marry him. . . But now they had taken Gerasim to Moscow, bought him boots, had him made a full-skirted coat for summer, a sheepskin for winter, put into his hand a broom and a spade, and appointed him porter.

At first he intensely disliked his new mode of life. From his childhood he had been used to field labor, to village life. Shut off by his affliction from the society of men, he had grown up, dumb and mighty, as a tree grows on a fruitful soil. When he was transported to the town, he could not understand what was being done with him; he was miserable and stupefied, with the stupefaction of some strong young bull, taken straight from the meadow, where the rich grass stood up to his belly, taken and put in the truck of a railway train, and there, while smoke and sparks and gusts of steam puff out upon the sturdy beast, he is whirled onwards, whirled along with loud roar and whistle, whither--God knows! What Gerasim had to do in his new duties seemed a mere trifle to him after his hard toil as a peasant; in half an hour all his work was done, and he would once more stand stock-still in the middle of the courtyard, staring open-mouthed at all the passers-by, as though trying to wrest from them the explanation of his perplexing position; or he would suddenly go off into some corner, and flinging a long way off the broom or the spade, throw himself on his face on the ground, and lie for hours together without stirring, like a caged beast. But man gets used to anything, and Gerasim got used at last to living in town. He had little work to do; his whole duty consisted in keeping the courtyard clean, bringing in a barrel of water twice a day, splitting and dragging in wood for the kitchen and the house, keeping out strangers, and watching at night. And it must be said he did his duty zealously. In his courtyard there was never a shaving lying about, never a speck of dust; if sometimes, in the muddy season, the wretched nag, put under his charge for fetching water, got stuck in the road, he would simply give it a shove with his shoulder, and set not only the cart but the horse itself moving. If he set to chopping wood, the axe fairly rang like glass, and chips and chunks flew in all directions. And as for strangers, after he had one night caught two thieves and knocked their heads together--knocked them so that there was not the slightest need to take them to the police-station afterwards--every one in the neighborhood began to feel a great respect for him; even those who came in the daytime, by no means robbers, but simply unknown persons, at the sight of the terrible porter, waved and shouted to him as though he could hear their shouts. With all the rest of the servants, Gerasim was on terms hardly friendly--they were afraid of him--but familiar; he regarded them as his fellows. They explained themselves to him by signs, and he understood them, and exactly carried out all orders, but knew his own rights too, and soon no one dared to take his seat at the table. Gerasim was altogether of a strict and serious temper, he liked order in everything; even the cocks did not dare to fight in his presence, or woe betide them! Directly he caught sight of them, he would seize them by the legs, swing them ten times round in the air like a wheel, and throw them in different directions. There were geese, too, kept in the yard; but the goose, as is well known, is a dignified and reasonable bird: Gerasim felt a respect for them, looked after them, and fed them; he was himself not unlike a gander of the steppes. He was assigned a little garret over the kitchen; he arranged it himself to his own liking, made a bedstead in it of oak boards on four stumps of wood for legs--a truly Titanic bedstead; one might have put a ton or two on it--it would not have bent under the load; under the bed was a solid chest; in a corner stood a little table of the same strong kind, and near the table a three-legged stool, so solid and squat that Gerasim himself would sometimes pick it up and drop it again with a smile of delight. The garret was locked up by means of a padlock that looked like a kalatch or basket-shaped loaf, only black; the key of this padlock Gerasim always carried about him in his girdle. He did not like people to come to his garret.

So passed a year, at the end of which a little incident befell Gerasim.

The old lady, in whose service he lived as porter, adhered in everything to the ancient ways, and kept a large number of servants. In her house were not only laundresses, sempstresses, carpenters, tailors and tailoresses, there was even a harness-maker--he was reckoned as a veterinary surgeon, too,--and a doctor for the servants; there was a household doctor for the mistress; there was, lastly, a shoemaker, by name Kapiton Klimov, a sad drunkard. Klimov regarded himself as an injured creature, whose merits were unappreciated, a cultivated man from Petersburg, who ought not to be living in Moscow without occupation--in the wilds, so to speak; and if he drank, as he himself expressed it emphatically, with a blow on his chest, it was sorrow drove him to it. So one day his mistress had a conversation about him with her head steward, Gavrila, a man whom, judging solely from his little yellow eyes and nose like a duck's beak, fate itself, it seemed, had marked out as a person in authority. The lady expressed her regret at the corruption of the morals of Kapiton, who had, only the evening before, been picked up somewhere in the street.

"Now, Gavrila," she observed, all of a sudden, "now, if we were to marry him, what do you think, perhaps he would be steadier?"

"Why not marry him, indeed, 'm? He could be married, 'm," answered Gavrila, "and it would be a very good thing, to be sure, 'm."

"Yes; only who is to marry him?"

"Ay, 'm. But that's at your pleasure, 'm. He may, any way, so to say, be wanted for something; he can't be turned adrift altogether."

"I fancy he likes Tatiana."

Gavrila was on the point of making some reply, but he shut his lips tightly.

"Yes! . . . let him marry Tatiana," the lady decided, taking a pinch of snuff complacently, "Do you hear?"

"Yes, 'm," Gavrila articulated, and he withdrew.

Returning to his own room (it was in a little lodge, and was almost filled up with metal-bound trunks), Gavrila first sent his wife away, and then sat down at the window and pondered. His mistress's unexpected arrangement had clearly put him in a difficulty. At last he got up and sent to call Kapiton. Kapiton made his appearance. . . But before reporting their conversation to the reader, we consider it not out of place to relate in few words who was this Tatiana, whom it was to be Kapiton's lot to marry, and why the great lady's order had disturbed the steward.

Tatiana, one of the laundresses referred to above (as a trained and skilful laundress she was in charge of the fine linen only), was a woman of twenty-eight, thin, fair-haired, with moles on her left cheek. Moles on the left cheek are regarded as of evil omen in Russia--a token of unhappy life. . . Tatiana could not boast of her good luck. From her earliest youth she had been badly treated; she had done the work of two, and had never known affection; she had been poorly clothed and had received the smallest wages. Relations she had practically none; an uncle she had once had, a butler, left behind in the country as useless, and other uncles of hers were peasants--that was all. At one time she had passed for a beauty, but her good looks were very soon over. In disposition, she was very meek, or, rather, scared; towards herself, she felt perfect indifference; of others, she stood in mortal dread; she thought of nothing but how to get her work done in good time, never talked to any one, and trembled at the very name of her mistress, though the latter scarcely knew her by sight. When Gerasim was brought from the country, she was ready to die with fear on seeing his huge figure, tried all she could to avoid meeting him, even dropped her eyelids when sometimes she chanced to run past him, hurrying from the house to the laundry. Gerasim at first paid no special attention to her, then he used to smile when she came his way, then he began even to stare admiringly at her, and at last he never took his eyes off her. She took his fancy, whether by the mild expression of her face or the timidity of her movements, who can tell? So one day she was stealing across the yard, with a starched dressing-jacket of her mistress's carefully poised on her outspread fingers . . . some one suddenly grasped her vigorously by the elbow; she turned round and fairly screamed; behind her stood Gerasim. With a foolish smile, making inarticulate caressing grunts, he held out to her a gingerbread cock with gold tinsel on his tail and wings. She was about to refuse it, but he thrust it forcibly into her hand, shook his head, walked away, and turning round, once more grunted something very affectionately to her.

From that day forward he gave her no peace; wherever she went, he was on the spot at once, coming to meet her, smiling, grunting, waving his hands; all at once he would pull a ribbon out of the bosom of his smock and put it in her hand, or would sweep the dust out of her way. The poor girl simply did not know how to behave or what to do. Soon the whole household knew of the dumb porter's wiles; jeers, jokes, sly hints, were showered upon Tatiana. At Gerasim, however, it was not every one who would dare to scoff; he did not like jokes; indeed, in his presence, she, too, was left in peace. Whether she liked it or not, the girl found herself to be under his protection. Like all deaf-mutes, he was very suspicious, and very readily perceived when they were laughing at him or at her. One day, at dinner, the wardrobe-keeper, Tatiana's superior, fell to nagging, as it is called, at her, and brought the poor thing to such a state that she did not know where to look, and was almost crying with vexation. Gerasim got up all of a sudden, stretched out his gigantic hand, laid it on the wardrobe-maid's head, and looked into her face with such grim ferocity that her head positively flopped upon the table. Every one was still. Gerasim took up his spoon again and went on with his cabbage-soup. "Look at him, the dumb devil, the wood-demon!" they all muttered in undertones, while the wardrobe-maid got up and went out into the maid's room. Another time, noticing that Kapiton--the same Kapiton who was the subject of the conversation reported above--was gossiping somewhat too attentively with Tatiana, Gerasim beckoned him to him, led him into the cartshed, and taking up a shaft that was standing in a corner by one end, lightly, but most significantly, menaced him with it. Since then no one addressed a word to Tatiana. And all this cost him nothing. It is true the wardrobe-maid, as soon as she reached the maids' room, promptly fell into a fainting fit, and behaved altogether so skilfully that Gerasim's rough action reached his mistress's knowledge the same day. But the capricious old lady only laughed, and several times, to the great offence of the wardrobe-maid, forced her to repeat "how he bent your head down with his heavy hand," and next day she sent Gerasim a rouble. She looked on him with favor as a strong and faithful watchman. Gerasim stood in considerable awe of her, but, all the same, he had hopes of her favor, and was preparing to go to her with a petition for leave to marry Tatiana. He was only waiting for a new coat, promised him by the steward, to present a proper appearance before his mistress, when this same mistress suddenly took it into her head to marry Tatiana to Kapiton.

The reader will now readily understand the perturbation of mind that overtook the steward Gavrila after his conversation with his mistress. "My lady," he thought, as he sat at the window, "favors Gerasim, to be sure"--(Gavrila was well aware of this, and that was why he himself looked on him with an indulgent eye)--"still he is a speechless creature. I could not, indeed, put it before the mistress that Gerasim's courting Tatiana. But, after all, it's true enough; he's a queer sort of husband. But on the other hand, that devil, God forgive me, has only got to find out they're marrying Tatiana to Kapiton, he'll smash up everything in the house, 'pon my soul! There's no reasoning with him; why, he's such a devil, God forgive my sins, there's no getting over him nohow . . . 'pon my soul!"

Kapiton's entrance broke the thread of Gavrila's reflections. The dissipated shoemaker came in, his hands behind him, and lounging carelessly against a projecting angle of the wall, near the door, crossed his right foot in front of his left, and tossed his head, as much as to say, "What do you want?"

Gavrila looked at Kapiton, and drummed with his fingers on the window-frame. Kapiton merely screwed up his leaden eyes a little, but he did not look down; he even grinned slightly, and passed his hand over his whitish locks which were sticking up in all directions. "Well, here I am. What is it?"

"You're a pretty fellow," said Gavrila, and paused. "A pretty fellow you are, there's no denying!"

Kapiton only twitched his little shoulders. "Are you any better, pray?" he thought to himself.

"Just look at yourself, now, look at yourself," Gavrila went on reproachfully; "now, whatever do you look like?"

Kapiton serenely surveyed his shabby, tattered coat and his patched trousers, and with special attention stared at his burst boots, especially the one on the tip-toe of which his right foot so gracefully poised, and he fixed his eyes again on the steward.

"Well?"

"Well?" repeated Gavrila. "Well? And then you say well? You look like Old Nick himself, God forgive my saying so, that's what you look like."

Kapiton blinked rapidly.

"Go on abusing me, go on, if you like, Gavrila Andreitch," he thought to himself again.

"Here you've been drunk again," Gavrila began, "drunk again, haven't you? Eh? Come, answer me!"

"Owing to the weakness of my health, I have exposed myself to spirituous beverages, certainly," replied Kapiton.

"Owing to the weakness of your health! . . . They let you off too easy, that's what it is; and you've been apprenticed in Petersburg. . . Much you learned in your apprenticeship! You simply eat your bread in idleness."

"In that matter, Gavrila Andreitch, there is One to judge me, the Lord God Himself, and no one else. He also knows what manner of man I be in this world, and whether I eat my bread in idleness. And as concerning your contention regarding drunkenness, in that matter, too, I am not to blame, but rather a friend; he led me into temptation, but was diplomatic and got away, while I . . ."

"While you were left like a goose, in the street. Ah, you're a dissolute fellow!

But that's not the point," the steward went on, "I've something to tell you. Our lady . . ." here he paused a minute, "it's our lady's pleasure that you should be married. Do you hear? She imagines you may be steadier when you're married. Do you understand?"

"To be sure I do."

"Well, then. For my part I think it would be better to give you a good hiding. But there--it's her business. Well? are you agreeable?"

Kapiton grinned.

"Matrimony is an excellent thing for any one, Gavrila Andreitch; and, as far as I am concerned, I shall be quite agreeable."

"Very well, then," replied Gavrila, while he reflected to himself: "There's no denying the man expresses himself very properly. Only there's one thing," he pursued aloud: "the wife our lady's picked out for you is an unlucky choice."

"Why, who is she, permit me to inquire?"

"Tatiana."

"Tatiana?"

And Kapiton opened his eyes, and moved a little away from the wall.

"Well, what are you in such a taking for? . . . Isn't she to your taste, hey?"

"Not to my taste, do you say, Gavrila Andreitch? She's right enough, a hard-working steady girl. . . But you know very well yourself, Gavrila Andreitch, why that fellow, that wild man of the woods, that monster of the steppes, he's after her, you know. . ."

"I know, mate, I know all about it," the butler cut him short in a tone of annoyance: "but there, you see . . ."

"But upon my soul, Gavrila Andreitch! why, he'll kill me, by God, he will, he'll crush me like some fly; why, he's got a fist--why, you kindly look yourself what a fist he's got; why, he's simply got a fist like Minin Pozharsky's. You see he's deaf, he beats and does not hear how he's beating! He swings his great fists, as if he's asleep. And there's no possibility of pacifying him; and for why? Why, because, as you know yourself, Gavrila Andreitch, he's deaf, and what's more, has no more wit than the heel of my foot. Why, he's a sort of beast, a heathen idol, Gavrila Andreitch, and worse . . . a block of wood; what have I done that I should have to suffer from him now? Sure it is, it's all over me now; I've knocked about, I've had enough to put up with, I've been battered like an earthenware pot, but still I'm a man, after all, and not a worthless pot."

"I know, I know, don't go talking away. . ."

"Lord, my God!" the shoemaker continued warmly, "when is the end? when, O Lord! A poor wretch I am, a poor wretch whose sufferings are endless! What a life, what a life mine's been come to think of it! In my young days, I was beaten by a German I was 'prentice to; in the prime of life beaten by my own countrymen, and last of all, in ripe years, see what I have been brought to. . ."

"Ugh, you flabby soul!" said Gavrila Andreitch. "Why do you make so many words about it?"

"Why, do you say, Gavrila Andreitch? It's not a beating I'm afraid of, Gavrila Andreitch. A gentleman may chastise me in private, but give me a civil word before folks, and I'm a man still; but see now, whom I've to do with . . ."

"Come, get along," Gavrila interposed impatiently. Kapiton turned away and staggered off.

"But, if it were not for him," the steward shouted after him, "you would consent for your part?"

"I signify my acquiescence," retorted Kapiton as he disappeared.

His fine language did not desert him, even in the most trying positions.

The steward walked several times up and down the room.

"Well, call Tatiana now," he said at last.

A few instants later, Tatiana had come up almost noiselessly, and was standing in the doorway.

"What are your orders, Gavrila Andreitch?" she said in a soft voice.

The steward looked at her intently.

"Well, Taniusha," he said, "would you like to be married? Our lady has chosen a husband for you?"

"Yes, Gavrila Andreitch. And whom has she deigned to name as a husband for me?" she added falteringly.

"Kapiton, the shoemaker."

"Yes, sir."

"He's a feather-brained fellow, that's certain. But it's just for that the mistress reckons upon you."

"Yes, sir."

"There's one difficulty . . . you know the deaf man, Gerasim, he's courting you, you see. How did you come to bewitch such a bear? But you see, he'll kill you, very like, he's such a bear . . ."

"He'll kill me, Gavrila Andreitch, he'll kill me, and no mistake."

"Kill you . . . Well we shall see about that. What do you mean by saying he'll kill you? Has he any right to kill you? tell me yourself."

"I don't know, Gavrila Andreitch, about his having any right or not."

"What a woman! why, you've made him no promise, I suppose . . ."

"What are you pleased to ask of me?"

The steward was silent for a little, thinking, "You're a meek soul! Well, that's right," he said aloud; "we'll have another talk with you later, now you can go, Taniusha; I see you're not unruly, certainly."

Tatiana turned, steadied herself a little against the doorpost, and went away.

"And, perhaps, our lady will forget all about this wedding by to- morrow," thought the steward; "and here am I worrying myself for nothing! As for that insolent fellow, we must tie him down if it comes to that, we must let the police know . . . Ustinya Fyedorovna!" he shouted in a loud voice to his wife, "heat the samovar, my good soul . . ." All that day Tatiana hardly went out of the laundry. At first she had started crying, then she wiped away her tears, and set to work as before. Kapiton stayed till late at night at the gin-shop with a friend of his, a man of gloomy appearance, to whom he related in detail how he used to live in Petersburg with a gentleman, who would have been all right, except he was a bit too strict, and he had a slight weakness besides, he was too fond of drink; and, as to the fair sex, he didn't stick at anything. His gloomy companion merely said yes; but when Kapiton announced at last that, in a certain event, he would have to lay hands on himself to-morrow, his gloomy companion remarked that it was bedtime. And they parted in surly silence.

Meanwhile, the steward's anticipations were not fulfilled. The old lady was so much taken up with the idea of Kapiton's wedding, that even in the night she talked of nothing else to one of her companions, who was kept in her house solely to entertain her in case of sleeplessness, and, like a night cabman, slept in the day. When Gavrila came to her after morning tea with his report, her first question was:

"And how about our wedding--is it getting on all right?" He replied, of course, that it was getting on first-rate, and that Kapiton would appear before her to pay his reverence to her that day. The old lady was not quite well; she did not give much time to business. The steward went back to his own room, and called a council. The matter certainly called for serious consideration. Tatiana would make no difficulty, of course; but Kapiton had declared in the hearing of all that he had but one head to lose, not two or three. . . Gerasim turned rapid sullen looks on every one, would not budge from the steps of the maids' quarters, and seemed to guess that some mischief was being hatched against him. They met together. Among them was an old sideboard waiter, nicknamed Uncle Tail, to whom every one looked respectfully for counsel, though all they got out of him was, "Here's a pretty pass! to be sure, to be sure, to be sure!" As a preliminary measure of security, to provide against contingencies, they locked Kapiton up in the lumber-room where the filter was kept; then considered the question with the gravest deliberation. It would, to be sure, be easy to have recourse to force. But Heaven save us! There would be an uproar, the mistress would be put out--it would be awful! What should they do? They thought and thought, and at last thought out a solution. It had many a time been observed that Gerasim could not bear drunkards. . . . As he sat at the gates, he would always turn away with disgust when some one passed by intoxicated, with unsteady steps and his cap on one side of his ear. They resolved that Tatiana should be instructed to pretend to be tipsy, and should pass by Gerasim staggering and reeling about. The poor girl refused for a long while to agree to this, but they persuaded her at last; she saw, too, that it was the only possible way of getting rid of her adorer. She went out. Kapiton was released from the lumber-room; for, after all, he had an interest in the affair. Gerasim was sitting on the curbstone at the gates, scraping the ground with a spade. . . . From behind every corner, from behind every window-blind, the others were watching him. . . . The trick succeeded beyond all expectations. On seeing Tatiana, at first, he nodded as usual, making caressing, inarticulate sounds; then he looked carefully at her, dropped his spade, jumped up, went up to her, brought his face close to her face. . . . In her fright she staggered more than ever, and shut her eyes. . . . He took her by the arm, whirled her right across the yard, and going into the room where the council had been sitting, pushed her straight at Kapiton. Tatiana fairly swooned away. . . . Gerasim stood, looked at her, waved his hand, laughed, and went off, stepping heavily, to his garret. . . . For the next twenty-four hours he did not come out of it. The postilion Antipka said afterwards that he saw Gerasim through a crack in the wall, sitting on his bedstead, his face in his hand. From time to time he uttered soft regular sounds; he was wailing a dirge, that is, swaying backwards and forwards with his eyes shut, and shaking his head as drivers or bargemen do when they chant their melancholy songs. Antipka could not bear it, and he came away from the crack. When Gerasim came out of the garret next day, no particular change could be observed in him. He only seemed, as it were, more morose, and took not the slightest notice of Tatiana or Kapiton. The same evening, they both had to appear before their mistress with geese under their arms, and in a week's time they were married. Even on the day of the wedding Gerasim showed no change of any sort in his behavior. Only, he came back from the river without water, he had somehow broken the barrel on the road; and at night, in the stable, he washed and rubbed down his horse so vigorously, it swayed like a blade of grass in the wind, and staggered from one leg to the other under his fists of iron.

All this had taken place in the spring. Another year passed by, during which Kapiton became a hopeless drunkard, and as being absolutely of no use for anything, was sent away with the store wagons to a distant village with his wife. On the day of his departure, he put a very good face on it at first, and declared that he would always be at home, send him where they would, even to the other end of the world; but later on he lost heart, began grumbling that he was being taken to uneducated people, and collapsed so completely at last that he could not even put his own hat on. Some charitable soul stuck it on his forehead, set the peak straight in front, and thrust it on with a slap from above. When everything was quite ready, and the peasants already held the reins in their hands, and were only waiting for the words "With God's blessing!" to start, Gerasim came out of his garret, went up to Tatiana, and gave her as a parting present a red cotton handkerchief he had bought for her a year ago. Tatiana, who had up to that instant borne all the revolting details of her life with great indifference, could not control herself upon that; she burst into tears, and as she took her seat in the cart, she kissed Gerasim three times like a good Christian. He meant to accompany her as far as the town-barrier, and did walk beside her cart for a while, but he stopped suddenly at the Crimean ford, waved his hand, and walked away along the riverside.

It was getting towards evening. He walked slowly, watching the water. All of a sudden he fancied something was floundering in the mud close to the bank. He stooped over, and saw a little white-and-black puppy, who, in spite of all its efforts, could not get out of the water; it was struggling, slipping back, and trembling all over its thin wet little body. Gerasim looked at the unlucky little dog, picked it up with one hand, put it into the bosom of his coat, and hurried with long steps homewards. He went into his garret, put the rescued puppy on his bed, covered it with his thick overcoat, ran first to the stable for straw, and then to the kitchen for a cup of milk. Carefully folding back the overcoat, and spreading out the straw, he set the milk on the bedstead. The poor little puppy was not more than three weeks old, its eyes were just open--one eye still seemed rather larger than the other; it did not know how to lap out of a cup, and did nothing but shiver and blink. Gerasim took hold of its head softly with two fingers, and dipped its little nose into the milk. The pup suddenly began lapping greedily, sniffing, shaking itself, and choking. Gerasim watched and watched it, and all at once he laughed outright. . . . All night long he was waiting on it, keeping it covered, and rubbing it dry. He fell asleep himself at last, and slept quietly and happily by its side.

No mother could have looked after her baby as Gerasim looked after his little nursling. At first she--for the pup turned out to be a bitch--was very weak, feeble, and ugly, but by degrees she grew stronger and improved in looks, and, thanks to the unflagging care of her preserver, in eight months' time she was transformed into a very pretty dog of the spaniel breed, with long ears, a bushy spiral tail, and large, expressive eyes. She was devotedly attached to Gerasim, and was never a yard from his side; she always followed him about wagging her tail. He had even given her a name--the dumb know that their inarticulate noises call the attention of others. He called her Mumu. All the servants in the house liked her, and called her Mumu, too. She was very intelligent, she was friendly with every one, but was only fond of Gerasim. Gerasim, on his side, loved her passionately, and he did not like it when other people stroked her; whether he was afraid for her, or jealous--God knows! She used to wake him in the morning, pulling at his coat; she used to take the reins in her mouth, and bring him up the old horse that carried the water, with whom she was on very friendly terms. With a face of great importance, she used to go with him to the river; she used to watch his brooms and spades, and never allowed any one to go into his garret. He cut a little hole in his door on purpose for her, and she seemed to feel that only in Gerasim's garret she was completely mistress and at home; and directly she went in, she used to jump with a satisfied air upon the bed. At night she did not sleep at all, but she never barked without sufficient cause, like some stupid house-dog, who, sitting on its hind-legs, blinking, with its nose in the air, barks simply from dullness, at the stars, usually three times in succession. No! Mumu's delicate little voice was never raised without good reason; either some stranger was passing close to the fence, or there was some suspicious sound or rustle somewhere. . . . In fact, she was an excellent watch-dog. It is true that there was another dog in the yard, a tawny old dog with brown spots, called Wolf, but he was never, even at night, let off the chain; and, indeed, he was so decrepit that he did not even wish for freedom. He used to lie curled up in his kennel, and only rarely uttered a sleepy, almost noiseless bark, which broke off at once, as though he were himself aware of its uselessness. Mumu never went into the mistress's house; and when Gerasim carried wood into the rooms, she always stayed behind, impatiently waiting for him at the steps, pricking up her ears and turning her head to right and to left at the slightest creak of the door . . .

So passed another year. Gerasim went on performing his duties as house- porter, and was very well content with his lot, when suddenly an unexpected incident occurred. . . . One fine summer day the old lady was walking up and down the drawing-room with her dependants. She was in high spirits; she laughed and made jokes. Her servile companions laughed and joked too, but they did not feel particularly mirthful; the household did not much like it, when their mistress was in a lively mood, for, to begin with, she expected from every one prompt and complete participation in her merriment, and was furious if any one showed a face that did not beam with delight; and secondly, these outbursts never lasted long with her, and were usually followed by a sour and gloomy mood. That day she had got up in a lucky hour; at cards she took the four knaves, which means the fulfilment of one's wishes (she used to try her fortune on the cards every morning), and her tea struck her as particularly delicious, for which her maid was rewarded by words of praise, and by twopence in money. With a sweet smile on her wrinkled lips, the lady walked about the drawing-room and went up to the window. A flower-garden had been laid out before the window, and in the very middle bed, under a rosebush, lay Mumu busily gnawing a bone. The lady caught sight of her.

"Mercy on us!" she cried suddenly; "what dog is that?"

The companion, addressed by the old lady, hesitated, poor thing, in that wretched state of uneasiness which is common in any person in a dependent position who doesn't know very well what significance to give to the exclamation of a superior.

"I d . . . d . . . don't know," she faltered; "I fancy it's the dumb man's dog."

"Mercy!" the lady cut her short; "but it's a charming little dog! order it to be brought in. Has he had it long? How is it I've never seen it before? . . . Order it to be brought in."

The companion flew at once into the hall.

"Boy, boy!" she shouted; "bring Mumu in at once! She's in the flower- garden."

"Her name's Mumu then," observed the lady; "a very nice name."

"Oh, very, indeed!" chimed in the companion. "Make haste, Stepan!"

Stepan, a sturdy-built young fellow, whose duties were those of a footman, rushed headlong into the flower-garden, and tried to capture Mumu, but she cleverly slipped from his fingers, and with her tail in the air, fled full speed to Gerasim, who was at that instant in the kitchen, knocking out and cleaning a barrel, turning it upside down in his hands like a child's drum. Stepan ran after her, and tried to catch her just at her master's feet; but the sensible dog would not let a stranger touch her, and with a bound, she got away. Gerasim looked on with a smile at all this ado; at last, Stepan got up, much amazed, and hurriedly explained to him by signs that the mistress wanted the dog brought in to her. Gerasim was a little astonished; he called Mumu, however, picked her up, and handed her over to Stepan. Stepan carried her into the drawing-room, and put her down on the parquette floor. The old lady began calling the dog to her in a coaxing voice. Mumu, who had never in her life been in such magnificent apartments, was very much frightened, and made a rush for the door, but, being driven back by the obsequious Stepan, she began trembling, and huddled close up against the wall.

"Mumu, Mumu, come to me, come to your mistress," said the lady; "come, silly thing . . . don't be afraid."

"Come, Mumu, come to the mistress," repeated the companions. "Come along!"

But Mumu looked round her uneasily, and did not stir.

"Bring her something to eat," said the old lady. "How stupid she is! she won't come to her mistress. What's she afraid of?"

"She's not used to your honor yet," ventured one of the companions in a timid and conciliatory voice.

Stepan brought in a saucer of milk, and set it down before Mumu, but Mumu would not even sniff at the milk, and still shivered, and looked round as before.

"Ah, what a silly you are!" said the lady, and going up to her, she stooped down, and was about to stroke her, but Mumu turned her head abruptly, and showed her teeth. The lady hurriedly drew back her hand. . . .

A momentary silence followed. Mumu gave a faint whine, as though she would complain and apologize. . . . The old lady moved back, scowling. The dog's sudden movement had frightened her.

"Ah!" shrieked all the companions at once, "she's not bitten you, has she? Heaven forbid! (Mumu had never bitten any one in her life.) Ah! ah!"

"Take her away," said the old lady in a changed voice. "Wretched little dog! What a spiteful creature!"

And, turning round deliberately, she went towards her boudoir. Her companions looked timidly at one another, and were about to follow her, but she stopped, stared coldly at them, and said, "What's that for, pray? I've not called you," and went out.

The companions waved their hands to Stepan in despair. He picked up Mumu, and flung her promptly outside the door, just at Gerasim's feet, and half an hour later a profound stillness led in the house, and the old lady sat on her sofa looking blacker than a thundercloud.

What trifles, if you think of it, will sometimes disturb any one!

Till evening the lady was out of humor; she did not talk to any one, did not play cards, and passed a bad night. She fancied the eau-de-Cologne they gave her was not the same as she usually had, and that her pillow smelt of soap, and she made the wardrobe-maid smell all the bed linen-- in fact she was very upset and cross altogether. Next morning she ordered Gavrila to be summoned an hour earlier than usual.

"Tell me, please," she began, directly the latter, not without some inward trepidation, crossed the threshold of her boudoir, "what dog was that barking all night in our yard? It wouldn't let me sleep!"

"A dog, 'm . . . what dog, 'm . . . may be, the dumb man's dog, 'm," he brought out in a rather unsteady voice.

"I don't know whether it was the dumb man's or whose, but it wouldn't let me sleep. And I wonder what we have such a lot of dogs for! I wish to know. We have a yard dog, haven't we?"

"Oh yes, 'm, we have, 'm. Wolf, 'm."

"Well, why more? what do we want more dogs for? It's simply introducing disorder. There's no one in control in the house--that's what it is. And what does the dumb man want with a dog? Who gave him leave to keep dogs in my yard? Yesterday I went to the window, and there it was lying in the flower-garden; it had dragged in nastiness it was gnawing, and my roses are planted there . . ."

The lady ceased.

"Let her be gone from to-day . . . do you hear?"

"Yes, 'm."

"To-day. Now go. I will send for you later for the report."

Gavrila went away.

As he went through the drawing-room, the steward, by way of maintaining order, moved a bell from one table to another; he stealthily blew his duck-like nose in the hall, and went into the outer-hall. In the outer- hall, on a locker, was Stepan asleep in the attitude of a slain warrior in a battalion picture, his bare legs thrust out below the coat which served him for a blanket. The steward gave him a shove, and whispered some instructions to him, to which Stepan responded with something between a yawn and a laugh. The steward went away, and Stepan got up, put on his coat and his boots, went out and stood on the steps. Five minutes had not passed before Gerasim made his appearance with a huge bundle of hewn logs on his back, accompanied by the inseparable Mumu. (The lady had given orders that her bed-room and boudoir should be heated at times even in the summer.) Gerasim turned sideways before the door, shoved it open with his shoulder, and staggered into the house with his load. Mumu, as usual, stayed behind to wait for him. Then Stepan, seizing his chance, suddenly pounced on her, like a kite on a chicken, held her down to the ground, gathered her up in his arms, and without even putting on his cap, ran out of the yard with her, got into the first fly he met, and galloped off to a market-place. There he soon found a purchaser, to whom he sold her for a shilling, on condition that he would keep her for at least a week tied up; then he returned at once. But before he got home, he got off the fly, and going right round the yard, jumped over the fence into the yard from a back street. He was afraid to go in at the gate for fear of meeting Gerasim.

His anxiety was unnecessary, however; Gerasim was no longer in the yard. On coming out of the house he had at once missed Mumu. He never remembered her failing to wait for his return, and began running up and down, looking for her, and calling her in his own way. . . . He rushed up to his garret, up to the hay-loft, ran out into the street, this way and that. . . . She was lost! He turned to the other serfs, with the most despairing signs, questioned them about her, pointing to her height from the ground, describing her with his hands. . . . Some of them really did not know what had become of Mumu, and merely shook their heads; others did know, and smiled to him for all response; while the steward assumed an important air, and began scolding the coachmen. Then Gerasim ran right away out of the yard.

It was dark by the time he came back. From his worn-out look, his unsteady walk, and his dusty clothes, it might be surmised that he had been running over half Moscow. He stood still opposite the windows of the mistress's house, took a searching look at the steps where a group of house-serfs were crowded together, turned away, and uttered once more his inarticulate "Mumu." Mumu did not answer. He went away. Every one looked after him, but no one smiled or said a word, and the inquisitive postilion Antipka reported next morning in the kitchen that the dumb man had been groaning all night.

All the next day Gerasim did not show himself, so that they were obliged to send the coachman Potap for water instead of him, at which the coachman Potap was anything but pleased. The lady asked Gavrila if her orders had been carried out. Gavrila replied that they had. The next morning Gerasim came out of his garret, and went about his work. He came in to his dinner, ate it, and went out again, without a greeting to any one. His face, which had always been lifeless, as with all deaf-mutes, seemed now to be turned to stone. After dinner he went out of the yard again, but not for long; he came back, and went straight up to the hay-loft. Night came on, a clear moonlight night. Gerasim lay breathing heavily, and incessantly turning from side to side. Suddenly he felt something pull at the skirt of his coat. He started, but did not raise his head, and even shut his eyes tighter. But again there was a pull, stronger than before; he jumped up before him, with an end of string round her neck, was Mumu, twisting and turning. A prolonged cry of delight broke from his speechless breast; he caught up Mumu, and hugged her tight in his arms, she licked his nose and eyes, and beard and moustache, all in one instant. . . . He stood a little, thought a minute, crept cautiously down from the hay-loft, looked round, and having satisfied himself that no one could see him, made his way successfully to his garret. Gerasim had guessed before that his dog had not got lost by her own doing, that she must have been taken away by the mistress's orders; the servants had explained to him by signs that his Mumu had snapped at her, and he determined to take his own measures. First he fed Mumu with a bit of bread, fondled her, and put her to bed, then he fell to meditating, and spent the whole night long in meditating how he could best conceal her. At last he decided to leave her all day in the garret, and only to come in now and then to see her, and to take her out at night. The hole in the door he stopped up effectually with his old overcoat, and almost before it was light he was already in the yard, as though nothing had happened, even--innocent guile!--the same expression of melancholy on his face. It did not even occur to the poor deaf man that Mumu would betray herself by her whining; in reality, everyone in the house was soon aware that the dumb man's dog had come back, and was locked up in his garret, but from sympathy with him and with her, and partly, perhaps, from dread of him, they did not let him know that they had found out his secret. The steward scratched his head, and gave a despairing wave of his head, as much as to say, "Well, well, God have mercy on him! If only it doesn't come to the mistress's ears!"

But the dumb man had never shown such energy as on that day; he cleaned and scraped the whole courtyard, pulled up every single weed with his own hand, tugged up every stake in the fence of the flower-garden, to satisfy himself that they were strong enough, and unaided drove them in again; in fact, he toiled and labored so that even the old lady noticed his zeal. Twice in the course of the day Gerasim went stealthily in to see his prisoner; when night came on, he lay down to sleep with her in the garret, not in the hay-loft, and only at two o'clock in the night he went out to take her a turn in the fresh air.

After walking about the courtyard a good while with her, he was just turning back, when suddenly a rustle was heard behind the fence on the side of the back street. Mumu pricked up her ears, growled--went up to the fence, sniffed, and gave vent to a loud shrill bark. Some drunkard had thought fit to take refuge under the fence for the night. At that very time the old lady had just fallen asleep after a prolonged fit of "nervous agitation"; these fits of agitation always overtook her after too hearty a supper. The sudden bark waked her up: her heart palpitated, and she felt faint. "Girls, girls!" she moaned. "Girls!" The terrified maids ran into her bedroom. "Oh, oh, I am dying!" she said, flinging her arms about in her agitation. "Again, that dog, again! . . . Oh, send for the doctor. They mean to be the death of me. . . . The dog, the dog again! Oh!" And she let her head fall back, which always signified a swoon. They rushed for the doctor, that is, for the household physician, Hariton. This doctor, whose whole qualification consisted in wearing soft-soled boots, knew how to feel the pulse delicately. He used to sleep fourteen hours out of the twenty-four, but the rest of the time he was always sighing, and continually dosing the old lady with cherrybay drops. This doctor ran up at once, fumigated the room with burnt feathers, and when the old lady opened her eyes, promptly offered her a wineglass of the hallowed drops on a silver tray. The old lady took them, but began again at once in a tearful voice complaining of the dog, of Gavrila, and of her fate, declaring that she was a poor old woman, and that every one had forsaken her, no one pitied her, every one wished her dead. Meanwhile the luckless Mumu had gone on barking, while Gerasim tried in vain to call her away, from the fence. "There . . . there . . . again," groaned the old lady, and once more she turned up the whites of her eyes. The doctor whispered to a maid, she rushed into the outer hall, and shook Stepan, he ran to wake Gavrila, Gavrila in a fury ordered the whole household to get up.

Gerasim turned round, saw lights and shadows moving in the windows, and with an instinct of coming trouble in his heart, put Mumu under his arm, ran into his garret, and locked himself in. A few minutes later five men were banging at his door, but feeling the resistance of the bolt, they stopped. Gavrila ran up in a fearful state of mind, and ordered them all to wait there and watch till morning. Then he flew off himself to the maids' quarter, and through an old companion, Liubov Liubimovna, with whose assistance he used to steal tea, sugar, and other groceries and to falsify the accounts, sent word to the mistress that the dog had unhappily run back from somewhere, but that to-morrow she should be killed, and would the mistress be so gracious as not to be angry and to overlook it. The old lady would probably not have been so soon appeased, but the doctor had in his haste given her fully forty drops instead of twelve. The strong dose of narcotic acted; in a quarter of an hour the old lady was in a sound and peaceful sleep; while Gerasim was lying with a white face on his bed, holding Mumu's mouth tightly shut.

Next morning the lady woke up rather late. Gavrila was waiting till she should be awake, to give the order for a final assault on Gerasim's stronghold, while he prepared himself to face a fearful storm. But the storm did not come off. The old lady lay in bed and sent for the eldest of her dependent companions.

"Liubov Liubimovna," she began in a subdued weak voice--she was fond of playing the part of an oppressed and forsaken victim; needless to say, every one in the house was made extremely uncomfortable at such times-- "Liubov Liubimovna, you see my position; go, my love, to Gavrila Andreitch, and talk to him a little. Can he really prize some wretched cur above the repose--the very life--of his mistress? I could not bear to think so," she added, with an expression of deep feeling. "Go, my love; be so good as to go to Gavrila Andreitch for me."

Liubov Liubimovna went to Gavrila's room. What conversation passed between them is not known, but a short time after, a whole crowd of people was moving across the yard in the direction of Gerasim's garret. Gavrila walked in front, holding his cap on with his hand, though there was no wind. The footmen and cooks were close behind him; Uncle Tail was looking out of a window, giving instructions, that is to say, simply waving his hands. At the rear there was a crowd of small boys skipping and hopping along; half of them were outsiders who had run up. On the narrow staircase leading to the garret sat one guard; at the door were standing two more with sticks. They began to mount the stairs, which they entirely blocked up. Gavrila went up to the door, knocked with his fist, shouting, "Open the door!"

A stifled bark was audible, but there was no answer.

"Open the door, I tell you," he repeated.

"But, Gavrila Andreitch," Stepan observed from below, "he's deaf, you know--he doesn't hear."

They all laughed.

"What are we to do?" Gavrila rejoined from above.

"Why, there's a hole there in the door," answered Stepan, "so you shake the stick in there."

Gavrila bent down.

"He's stuffed it up with a coat or something."

"Well, you just push the coat in."

At this moment a smothered bark was heard again.

"See, see--she speaks for herself," was remarked in the crowd, and again they laughed.

Gavrila scratched his ear.

"No, mate," he responded at last, "you can poke the coat in yourself, if you like."

"All right, let me."

And Stepan scrambled up, took the stick, pushed in the coat, and began waving the stick about in the opening, saying, "Come out, come out!" as he did so. He was still waving the stick, when suddenly the door of the garret was flung open; all the crowd flew pell-mell down the stairs instantly, Gavrila first of all. Uncle Tail locked the window.

"Come, come, come," shouted Gavrila from the yard, "mind what you're about."

Gerasim stood without stirring in his doorway. The crowd gathered at the foot of the stairs. Gerasim, with his arms akimbo, looked down at all these poor creatures in German coats; in his red peasant's shirt he looked like a giant before them. Gavrila took a step forward.

"Mind, mate," said he, "don't be insolent."

And he began to explain to him by signs that the mistress insists on having his dog; that he must hand it over at once, or it would be the worse for him.

Gerasim looked at him, pointed to the dog, made a motion with his hand round his neck, as though he were pulling a noose tight, and glanced with a face of inquiry at the steward.

"Yes, yes," the latter assented, nodding; "yes, just so."

Gerasim dropped his eyes, then all of a sudden roused himself and pointed to Mumu, who was all the while standing beside him, innocently wagging her tail and pricking up her ears inquisitively. Then he repeated the strangling action round his neck and significantly struck himself on the breast, as though announcing he would take upon himself the task of killing Mumu.

"But you'll deceive us," Gavrila waved back in response.

Gerasim looked at him, smiled scornfully, struck himself again on the breast, and slammed to the door.

They all looked at one another in silence.

"What does that mean?" Gavrila began. "He's locked himself in."

"Let him be, Gavrila Andreitch," Stepan advised; "he'll do it if he's promised. He's like that, you know. . . . If he makes a promise, it's a certain thing. He's not like us others in that. The truth's the truth with him. Yes, indeed."

"Yes," they all repeated, nodding their heads, "yes--that's so--yes."

Uncle Tail opened his window, and he too said, "Yes."

"Well, may be, we shall see," responded Gavrila; "any way, we won't take off the guard. Here you, Eroshka!" he added, addressing a poor fellow in a yellow nankeen coat, who considered himself to be a gardener, "what have you to do? Take a stick and sit here, and if anything happens, run to me at once!"

Eroshka took a stick, and sat down on the bottom stair. The crowd dispersed, all except a few inquisitive small boys, while Gavrila went home and sent word through Liubov Liubimovna to the mistress that everything had been done, while he sent a postilion for a policeman in case of need. The old lady tied a knot in her handkerchief, sprinkled some eau-de-Cologne on it, sniffed at it, and rubbed her temples with it, drank some tea, and, being still under the influence of the cherrybay drops, fell asleep again.

An hour after all this hubbub the garret door opened, and Gerasim showed himself. He had on his best coat; he was leading Mumu by a string. Eroshka moved aside and let him pass. Gerasim went to the gates. All the small boys in the yard stared at him in silence. He did not even turn round; he only put his cap on in the street. Gavrila sent the same Eroshka to follow him and keep watch on him as a spy. Eroshka, seeing from a distance that he had gone into a cookshop with his dog, waited for him to come out again.

Gerasim was well known at the cookshop, and his signs were understood. He asked for cabbage soup with meat in it, and sat down with his arms on the table. Mumu stood beside his chair, looking calmly at him with her intelligent eyes. Her coat was glossy; one could see she had just been combed down. They brought

Gerasim the soup. He crumbled some bread into it, cut the meat up small, and put the plate on the ground. Mumu began eating in her usual refined way, her little muzzle daintily held so as scarcely to touch her food. Gerasim gazed a long while at her; two big tears suddenly rolled from his eyes; one fell on the dog's brow, the other into the soup. He shaded his face with his hand. Mumu ate up half the plate-ful, and came away from it, licking her lips. Gerasim got up, paid for the soup, and went out, followed by the rather perplexed glances of the waiter. Eroshka, seeing Gerasim, hid round a corner, and letting him get in front, followed him again.

Gerasim walked without haste, still holding Mumu by a string. When he got to the corner of the street, he stood still as though reflecting, and suddenly set off with rapid steps to the Crimean Ford. On the way he went into the yard of a house, where a lodge was being built, and carried away two bricks under his arm. At the Crimean Ford, he turned along the bank, went to a place where there were two lit-tle rowing-boats fastened to stakes (he had noticed them there before), and jumped into one of them with Mumu. A lame old man came out of a shed in the corner of a kitchen-garden and shouted after him; but Gerasim only nodded, and began rowing so vigorously, though against stream, that in an instant he had darted two hundred yards way. The old man stood for a while, scratched his back first with the left and then with the right hand, and went back hobbling to the shed.

Gerasim rowed on and on. Moscow was soon left behind. Meadows stretched each side of the bank, market gardens, fields, and copses; peasants' huts began to make their appearance. There was the fragrance of the country. He threw down his oars, bent his head down to Mumu, who was sitting facing him on a dry cross seat--the bottom of the boat was full of water--and stayed motionless, his mighty hands clasped upon her back, while the boat was gradually carried back by the cur-rent towards the town. At last Gerasim drew himself up hurriedly, with a sort of sick anger in his face, he tied up the bricks he had taken with string, made a running noose, put it round Mumu's neck, lifted her up over the river, and for the last time looked at her. . . . She watched him confidingly and without any fear, faintly wag-ging her tail. He turned away, frowned, and wrung his hands. . . . Gerasim heard nothing, neither the quick shrill whine of Mumu as she fell, nor the heavy splash of the water; for him the noisiest day was soundless and silent as even the stillest night is not silent to us. When he opened his eyes again, little wavelets were hurrying over the river, chasing one another; as before they broke against the boat's side, and only far away behind wide circles moved widening to the bank.

Directly Gerasim had vanished from Eroshka's sight, the latter returned home and reported what he had seen.

"Well, then," observed Stepan, "he'll drown her. Now we can feel easy about it. If he once promises a thing . . ."

No one saw Gerasim during the day. He did not have dinner at home. Evening came on; they were all gathered together to supper, except him.

"What a strange creature that Gerasim is!" piped a fat laundrymaid; "fancy, upsetting himself like that over a dog. . . . Upon my word!"

"But Gerasim has been here," Stepan cried all at once, scraping up his porridge with a spoon.

"How? when?"

"Why, a couple of hours ago. Yes, indeed! I ran against him at the gate; he was going out again from here; he was coming out of the yard. I tried to ask him about his dog, but he wasn't in the best of humors, I could see. Well, he gave me a shove; I suppose he only meant to put me out of his way, as if he'd say, 'Let me go, do!' but he fetched me such a crack on my neck, so seriously, that--oh! oh!" And Stepan, who could not help laughing, shrugged up and rubbed the back of his head. "Yes," he added; "he has got a fist; it's something like a fist, there's no denying that!"

They all laughed at Stepan, and after supper they separated to go to bed.

Meanwhile, at that very time, a gigantic figure with a bag on his shoulders and a stick in his hand, was eagerly and persistently stepping out along the T--- high-road. It was Gerasim. He was hurrying on without looking round; hurrying home-wards, to his own village, to his own country. After drowning poor Mumu, he had run back to his garret, hurriedly packed a few things together in an old horsecloth, tied it up in a bundle, tossed it on his shoulder, and so was ready. He had noticed the road carefully when he was brought to Moscow; the village his mistress had taken him from lay only about twenty miles off the high-road. He walked along it with a sort of invincible purpose, a desperate and at the same time joyous determination. He walked, his shoulders thrown back and his chest expanded; his eyes were fixed greedily straight before him. He hastened as though his old mother were waiting for him at home, as though she were calling him to her after long wanderings in strange parts, among strangers. The summer night, that was just drawing in, was still and warm; on one side, where the sun had set, the horizon was still light and faintly flushed with the last glow of the vanished day; on the other side a blue-gray twilight had already risen up. The night was coming up from that quarter. Quails were in hundreds around; corncrakes were calling to one another in the thickets. . . . Gerasim could not hear them; he could not hear the delicate night-whispering of the trees, by which his strong legs carried him, but he smelt the familiar scent of the ripening rye, which was wafted from the dark fields; he felt the wind, flying to meet him--the wind from home--beat caressingly upon his face, and play with his hair and his beard. He saw before him the whitening road homewards, straight as an arrow. He saw in the sky stars innumerable, lighting up his way, and stepped out, strong and bold as a lion, so that when the rising sun shed its moist rosy light upon the still fresh and unwearied traveller, already thirty miles lay between him and Moscow.

In a couple of days he was at home, in his little hut, to the great astonishment of the soldier's wife who had been put in there. After praying before the holy pictures, he set off at once to the village elder. The village elder was at first surprised; but the hay-cutting had just begun; Gerasim was a first-rate mower, and they put a scythe into his hand on the spot, and he went to mow in his old way, mowing so that the peasants were fairly astounded as they watched his wide sweeping strokes and the heaps he raked together. . . .

In Moscow the day after Gerasim's flight they missed him. They went to his garret, rummaged about in it, and spoke to Gavrila. He came, looked, shrugged his shoulders, and decided that the dumb man had either run away or had drowned himself with his stupid dog. They gave information to the police, and informed the lady. The old lady was furious, burst into tears, gave orders that he was to be found whatever happened, declared she had never ordered the dog to be destroyed, and, in fact, gave Gavrila such a rating that he could do nothing all day but shake his head and murmur, "Well!" until Uncle Tail checked him at last, sympathetically echoing "We-ell!" At last the news came from the country of Gerasim's being there. The old lady was somewhat pacified; at first she issued a mandate for him to be brought back without delay to Moscow; afterwards, however, she declared that such an ungrateful creature was absolutely of no use to her. Soon after this she died herself; and her heirs had no thought to spare for Gerasim; they let their mother's other servants redeem their freedom on payment of an annual rent.

And Gerasim is living still, a lonely man in his lonely hut; he is strong and healthy as before, and does the work of four men as before, and as before is serious and steady. But his neighbors have observed that ever since his return from Moscow he has quite given up the society of women; he will not even look at them, and does not keep even a single dog.

"It's his good luck, though," the peasants reason, "that he can get on without female folk; and as for a dog--what need has he of a dog? you wouldn't get a thief to go into his yard for any money!" Such is the fame of the dumb man's Titanic strength.

THE SHOT
BY
ALEXANDER POUSHKIN

From "Poushkin's Prose Tales." Translated by T. Keane.

CHAPTER I.

We were stationed in the little town of N--. The life of an officer in the army is well known. In the morning, drill and the riding-school; dinner with the Colonel or at a Jewish restaurant; in the evening, punch and cards. In N--- there was not one open house, not a single marriageable girl. We used to meet in each other's rooms, where, except our uniforms, we never saw anything.

One civilian only was admitted into our society. He was about thirty- five years of age, and therefore we looked upon him as an old fellow. His experience gave him great advantage over us, and his habitual taciturnity, stern disposition, and caustic tongue produced a deep impression upon our young minds. Some mystery sur-rounded his existence; he had the appearance of a Russian, although his name was a foreign one. He had formerly served in the Hussars, and with distinction. No-body knew the cause that had induced him to retire from the service and settle in a wretched little village, where he lived poorly and, at the same time, extravagantly. He always went on foot, and constantly wore a shabby black overcoat, but the of-ficers of our regiment were ever welcome at his table. His dinners, it is true, never consisted of more than two or three dishes, prepared by a retired soldier, but the champagne flowed like water. Nobody knew what his circumstances were, or what his income was, and nobody dared to question him about them. He had a collection of books, consisting chiefly of works on military matters and a few novels. He willingly lent them to us to read, and never asked for them back; on the other hand, he never returned to the owner the books that were lent to him. His principal amusement was shooting with a pistol. The walls of his room were riddled with bullets, and were as full of holes as a honeycomb. A rich collection of pistols was the only luxury in the humble cottage where he lived. The skill which he had acquired with his favorite weapon was simply incredible: and if he had offered to shoot a pear off somebody's forage-cap, not a man in our regiment would have hesitated to place the object upon his head.

Our conversation often turned upon duels. Silvio--so I will call him-- never joined in it. When asked if he had ever fought, he dryly replied that he had; but he entered into no particulars, and it was evident that such questions were not to his liking. We came to the conclusion that he had upon his conscience the memory of some unhappy victim of his terrible skill. Moreover, it never entered into the head of any of us to suspect him of anything like cowardice. There are persons whose mere look is sufficient to repel such a suspicion. But an unexpected incident occurred which astounded us all.

One day, about ten of our officers dined with Silvio. They drank as usual, that is to say, a great deal. After dinner we asked our host to hold the bank for a game at faro. For a long time he refused, for he hardly ever played, but at last he ordered cards to be brought, placed half a hundred ducats upon the table, and sat down to deal. We took our places round him, and the play began. It was Silvio's custom to preserve a complete silence when playing. He never disputed, and never entered into explanations. If the punter made a mistake in calculating, he immediately paid him the difference or noted down the surplus. We were acquainted with this habit of his, and we always allowed him to have his own way; but among us on this occasion was an officer who had only recently been transferred to our regiment. During the course of the game, this officer absently scored one point too many. Silvio took the chalk and noted down the correct account according to his usual custom. The officer, thinking that he had made a mistake, began to enter into explanations.

Silvio continued dealing in silence. The officer, losing patience, took the brush and rubbed out what he considered was wrong. Silvio took the chalk and corrected the score again. The officer, heated with wine, play, and the laughter of his comrades, considered himself grossly insulted, and in his rage he seized a brass candlestick from the table, and hurled it at Silvio, who barely succeeded in avoiding the missile. We were filled with consternation. Silvio rose, white with rage, and with gleaming eyes, said:

"My dear sir, have the goodness to withdraw, and thank God that this has happened in my house."

None of us entertained the slightest doubt as to what the result would be, and we already looked upon our new comrade as a dead man. The officer withdrew, saying that he was ready to answer for his offence in whatever way the banker liked. The play went on for a few minutes longer, but feeling that our host was no longer interested in the game, we withdrew one after the other, and repaired to our respective quarters, after having exchanged a few words upon the probability of there soon being a vacancy in the regiment.

The next day, at the riding-school, we were already asking each other if the poor lieutenant was still alive, when he himself appeared among us. We put the same question to him, and he replied that he had not yet heard from Silvio. This astonished us. We went to Silvio's house and found him in the courtyard shooting bullet after bullet into an ace pasted upon the gate. He received us as usual, but did not utter a word about the event of the previous evening. Three days passed, and the lieutenant was still alive. We asked each other in astonishment: "Can it be possible that Silvio is not going to fight?"

Silvio did not fight. He was satisfied with a very lame explanation, and became reconciled to his assailant.

This lowered him very much in the opinion of all our young fellows. Want of courage is the last thing to be pardoned by young men, who usually look upon bravery as the chief of all human virtues, and the excuse for every possible fault. But, by degrees, everything became forgotten, and Silvio regained his former influence.

I alone could not approach him on the old footing. Being endowed by nature with a romantic imagination, I had become attached more than all the others to the man whose life was an enigma, and who seemed to me the hero of some mysterious drama. He was fond of me; at least, with me alone did he drop his customary sarcastic tone, and converse on different subjects in a simple and unusually agreeable manner. But after this unlucky evening, the thought that his honor had been tarnished, and that the stain had been allowed to remain upon it in accordance with his own wish, was ever present in my mind, and prevented me treating him as before. I was ashamed to look at him. Silvio was too intelligent and experienced not to observe this and guess the cause of it. This seemed to vex him; at least I observed once or twice a desire on his part to enter into an explanation with me, but I avoided such opportunities, and Silvio gave up the attempt. From that time forward I saw him only in the presence of my comrades, and our confidential conversations came to an end.

The inhabitants of the capital, with minds occupied by so many matters of business and pleasure, have no idea of the many sensations so familiar to the inhabitants of villages and small towns, as, for instance, the awaiting the arrival of the post. On Tuesdays and Fridays our regimental bureau used to be filled with officers: some expecting money, some letters, and others newspapers. The packets were usually opened on the spot, items of news were communicated from one to another, and the bureau used to present a very animated picture. Silvio used to have his letters addressed to our regiment, and he was generally there to receive them.

One day he received a letter, the seal of which he broke with a look of great impatience. As he read the contents, his eyes sparkled. The officers, each occupied with his own letters, did not observe anything.

"Gentlemen," said Silvio, "circumstances demand my immediate departure; I leave to-night. I hope that you will not refuse to dine with me for the last time. I shall expect you, too," he added, turning towards me. "I shall expect you without fail."

With these words he hastily departed, and we, after agreeing to meet at Silvio's, dispersed to our various quarters.

I arrived at Silvio's house at the appointed time, and found nearly the whole regiment there. All his things were already packed; nothing remained but the bare, bullet-riddled walls. We sat down to table. Our host was in an excellent humor, and his gayety was quickly communicated to the rest. Corks popped every moment, glasses foamed incessantly, and, with the utmost warmth, we wished our departing friend a pleasant journey and every happiness. When we rose from the table it was already late in the evening. After having wished everybody good-bye, Silvio took me by the hand and detained me just at the moment when I was preparing to depart.

"I want to speak to you," he said in a low voice.

I stopped behind.

The guests had departed, and we two were left alone. Sitting down opposite each other, we silently lit our pipes. Silvio seemed greatly troubled; not a trace remained of his former convulsive gayety. The intense pallor of his face, his sparkling eyes, and the thick smoke issuing from his mouth, gave him a truly diabolical appearance. Several minutes elapsed, and then Silvio broke the silence.

"Perhaps we shall never see each other again," said he; "before we part, I should like to have an explanation with you. You may have observed that I care very little for the opinion of other people, but I like you, and I feel that it would be painful to me to leave you with a wrong impression upon your mind."

He paused, and began to knock the ashes out of his pipe. I sat gazing silently at the ground.

"You thought it strange," he continued, "that I did not demand satisfaction from that drunken idiot R---. You will admit, however, that having the choice of weapons, his life was in my hands, while my own was in no great danger. I could ascribe my forbearance to generosity alone, but I will not tell a lie. If I could have chastised R--- without the least risk to my own life, I should never have pardoned him."

I looked at Silvio with astonishment. Such a confession completely astounded me. Silvio continued:

"Exactly so: I have no right to expose myself to death. Six years ago I received a slap in the face, and my enemy still lives."

My curiosity was greatly excited.

"Did you not fight with him?" I asked. "Circumstances probably separated you."

"I did fight with him," replied Silvio; "and here is a souvenir of our duel."

Silvio rose and took from a cardboard box a red cap with a gold tassel and embroidery (what the French call a bonnet de police); he put it on-- a bullet had passed through it about an inch above the forehead.

"You know," continued Silvio, "that I served in one of the Hussar regiments. My character is well known to you: I am accustomed to taking the lead. From my youth this has been my passion. In our time dissoluteness was the fashion, and I was the most outrageous man in the army. We used to boast of our drunkenness; I beat in a drinking bout the famous Bourtsoff[1], of whom Denis Davidoff[2] has sung. Duels in our regiment were constantly taking place, and in all of them I was either second or principal. My comrades adored me, while the regimental commanders, who were constantly being changed, looked upon me as a necessary evil.

"I was calmly enjoying my reputation, when a young man belonging to a wealthy and distinguished family--I will not mention his name--joined our regiment. Never in my life have I met with such a fortunate fellow! Imagine to yourself youth, wit, beauty, unbounded gayety, the most reckless bravery, a famous name, untold wealth--imagine all these, and you can form some idea of the effect that he would be sure to produce among us. My supremacy was shaken. Dazzled by my reputation, he began to seek my friendship, but I received him coldly, and without the least regret he held aloof from me. I took a hatred to him. His success in the regiment and in the society of ladies brought me to the verge of despair. I began to seek a quarrel with him; to my epigrams he replied with epigrams which always seemed to me more spontaneous and more cutting than mine, and which were decidedly more amusing, for he joked while I fumed. At last, at a ball given by a Polish landed proprietor, seeing him the object of the attention of all the ladies, and especially of the mistress of the house, with whom I was upon very good terms, I whispered some grossly insulting remark in his ear. He flamed up and gave me a slap in the face. We grasped our swords; the ladies fainted; we were separated; and that same night we set out to fight.

"The dawn was just breaking. I was standing at the appointed place with my three seconds. With inexplicable impatience I awaited my opponent. The spring sun rose, and it was already growing hot. I saw him coming in the distance. He was walking on foot, accompanied by one second. We advanced to meet him. He approached, holding his cap filled with black cherries. The seconds measured twelve paces for us. I had to fire first, but my agitation was so great, that I could not

1   A cavalry officer, notorious for his drunken escapades
2   A military poet who flourished in the reign of Alexander I

depend upon the steadiness of my hand; and in order to give myself time to become calm, I ceded to him the first shot. My adversary would not agree to this. It was decided that we should cast lots. The first number fell to him, the constant favorite of fortune. He took aim, and his bullet went through my cap. It was now my turn. His life at last was in my hands; I looked at him eagerly, endeavoring to detect if only the faintest shadow of uneasiness. But he stood in front of my pistol, picking out the ripest cherries from his cap and spitting out the stones, which flew almost as far as my feet. His indifference annoyed me beyond measure. 'What is the use,' thought I, 'of depriving him of life, when he attaches no value whatever to it?' A malicious thought flashed through my mind. I lowered my pistol.

"'You don't seem to be ready for death just at present,' I said to him: 'you wish to have your breakfast; I do not wish to hinder you.'

"'You are not hindering me in the least,' replied he. 'Have the goodness to fire, or just as you please--the shot remains yours; I shall always be ready at your service.'

"I turned to the seconds, informing them that I had no intention of firing that day, and with that the duel came to an end.

"I resigned my commission and retired to this little place. Since then not a day has passed that I have not thought of revenge. And now my hour has arrived."

Silvio took from his pocket the letter that he had received that morning, and gave it to me to read. Some one (it seemed to be his business agent) wrote to him from Moscow, that a CERTAIN PERSON was going to be married to a young and beautiful girl.

"You can guess," said Silvio, "who the certain person is. I am going to Moscow. We shall see if he will look death in the face with as much indifference now, when he is on the eve of being married, as he did once with his cherries!"

With these words, Silvio rose, threw his cap upon the floor, and began pacing up and down the room like a tiger in his cage. I had listened to him in silence; strange conflicting feelings agitated me.

The servant entered and announced that the horses were ready. Silvio grasped my hand tightly, and we embraced each other. He seated himself in his telega, in which lay two trunks, one containing his pistols, the other his effects. We said good-bye once more, and the horses galloped off.

CHAPTER II.

Several years passed, and family circumstances compelled me to settle in the poor little village of M---. Occupied with agricultural pursuits, I ceased not to sigh in secret for my former noisy and careless life. The most difficult thing of all was having to accustom myself to passing the spring and winter evenings in perfect solitude. Until the hour for dinner I managed to pass away the time somehow or other, talking with the bailiff, riding about to inspect the work, or going round to look at the new buildings; but as soon as it began to get dark, I positively did not know what to do with myself. The few books that I had found in the cupboards and storerooms I already knew by heart. All the stories that my housekeeper Kirilovna could remember I had heard over and over again. The songs of the peasant women made me feel depressed. I tried drinking spirits, but it made my head ache; and moreover, I confess I was afraid of becoming a drunkard from mere chagrin, that is to say, the saddest kind of drunkard, of which I had seen many examples in our district.

I had no near neighbors, except two or three topers, whose conversation consisted for the most part of hiccups and sighs. Solitude was preferable to their society. At last I decided to go to bed as early as possible, and to dine as late as possible; in this way I shortened the evening and lengthened out the day, and I found that the plan answered very well.

Four versts from my house was a rich estate belonging to the Countess B---; but nobody lived there except the steward. The Countess had only visited her estate once, in the first year of her married life, and then she had remained there no longer than a month. But in the second spring of my hermitical life a report was circulated that the Countess, with her husband, was coming to spend the summer on her estate. The report turned out to be true, for they arrived at the beginning of June.

The arrival of a rich neighbor is an important event in the lives of country people. The landed proprietors and the people of their households talk about it for two months beforehand and for three years afterwards. As for me, I must confess that the news of the arrival of a young and beautiful neighbor affected me strongly. I burned with impatience to see her, and the first Sunday after her arrival I set out after dinner for the village of A---, to pay my respects to the Countess and her husband, as their nearest neighbor and most humble servant. A lackey conducted me into the Count's study, and then went to announce me. The spacious apartment was furnished with every possible luxury. Around the walls were cases filled with books and surmounted by bronze busts; over the marble mantelpiece was a large mirror; on the floor was a green cloth covered with carpets. Unaccustomed to luxury in my own poor corner, and not having seen the wealth of other people for a long time, I awaited the appearance of the Count with some little trepidation, as a suppliant from the provinces awaits the arrival of the minister. The door opened, and a handsome-looking man, of about thirty- two years of age, entered the room. The Count approached me with a frank and friendly air; I endeavored to be self-possessed and began to introduce myself, but he anticipated me. We sat down. His conversation, which was easy and agreeable, soon dissipated my awkward bashfulness; and I was already beginning to recover my usual composure, when the Countess suddenly entered, and I became more confused than ever. She was indeed beautiful. The Count presented me. I wished to appear at ease, but the more I tried to assume an air of unconstraint, the more awkward I felt. They, in order to give me time to recover myself and to become accustomed to my new acquaintances, began to talk to each other, treating me as a good neighbor, and without ceremony. Meanwhile, I walked about the room, examining the books and pictures. I am no judge of pictures, but one of them attracted my attention. It represented some view in Switzerland, but it was not the painting that struck me, but the circumstance that the canvas was shot through by two bullets, one planted just above the other.

"A good shot that!" said I, turning to the Count.

"Yes," replied he, "a very remarkable shot. . . . Do you shoot well?" he continued.

"Tolerably," replied I, rejoicing that the conversation had turned at last upon a subject that was familiar to me. "At thirty paces I can manage to hit a card without fail,--I mean, of course, with a pistol that I am used to."

"Really?" said the Countess, with a look of the greatest interest. "And you, my dear, could you hit a card at thirty paces?"

"Some day," replied the Count, "we will try. In my time I did not shoot badly, but it is now four years since I touched a pistol."

"Oh!" I observed, "in that case, I don't mind laying a wager that Your Excellency will not hit the card at twenty paces; the pistol demands practice every day. I know that from experience. In our regiment I was reckoned one of the best shots. It once happened that I did not touch a pistol for a whole month, as I had sent mine to be mended; and would you believe it, Your Excellency, the first time I began to shoot again, I missed a bottle four times in succession at twenty paces. Our captain, a witty and amusing fellow, happened to be standing by, and he said to me: 'It is evident, my friend, that your hand will not lift itself against the bottle.' No, Your Excellency, you must not neglect to practise, or your hand will soon lose its cunning. The best shot that I ever met used to shoot at least three times every day before dinner. It was as much his custom to do this as it was to drink his daily glass of brandy."

The Count and Countess seemed pleased that I had begun to talk.

"And what sort of a shot was he?" asked the Count.

"Well, it was this way with him, Your Excellency: if he saw a fly settle on the wall--you smile, Countess, but, before Heaven, it is the truth-- if he saw a fly, he would call out: 'Kouzka, my pistol!' Kouzka would bring him a loaded pistol--bang! and the fly would be crushed against the wall."

"Wonderful!" said the Count. "And what was his name?"

"Silvio, Your Excellency."

"Silvio!" exclaimed the Count, starting up. "Did you know Silvio?"

"How could I help knowing him, Your Excellency: we were intimate friends; he was received in our regiment like a brother officer, but it is now five years since I had any tidings of him. Then Your Excellency also knew him?"

"Oh, yes, I knew him very well. Did he ever tell you of one very strange incident in his life?"

"Does Your Excellency refer to the slap in the face that he received from some blackguard at a ball?"

"Did he tell you the name of this blackguard?"

"No, Your Excellency, he never mentioned his name, . . . Ah! Your Excellency!" I continued, guessing the truth: "pardon me . . . I did not know . . . could it really have been you?"

"Yes, I myself," replied the Count, with a look of extraordinary agitation; "and that bullet-pierced picture is a memento of our last meeting."

"Ah, my dear," said the Countess, "for Heaven's sake, do not speak about that; it would be too terrible for me to listen to."

"No," replied the Count: "I will relate everything. He knows how I insulted his friend, and it is only right that he should know how Silvio revenged himself."

The Count pushed a chair towards me, and with the liveliest interest I listened to the following story:

"Five years ago I got married. The first month--the honeymoon--I spent here, in this village. To this house I am indebted for the happiest moments of my life, as well as for one of its most painful recollections.

"One evening we went out together for a ride on horseback. My wife's horse became restive; she grew frightened, gave the reins to me, and returned home on foot. I rode on before. In the courtyard I saw a travelling carriage, and I was told that in my study sat waiting for me a man, who would not give his name, but who merely said that he had business with me. I entered the room and saw in the darkness a man, covered with dust and wearing a beard of several days' growth. He was standing there, near the fireplace. I approached him, trying to remember his features.

"'You do not recognize me, Count?' said he, in a quivering voice.

"'Silvio!' I cried, and I confess that I felt as if my hair had suddenly stood on end.

"'Exactly,' continued he. 'There is a shot due to me, and I have come to discharge my pistol. Are you ready?'

"His pistol protruded from a side pocket. I measured twelve paces and took my stand there in that corner, begging him to fire quickly, before my wife arrived. He hesitated, and asked for a light. Candles were brought in. I closed the doors, gave orders that nobody was to enter, and again begged him to fire. He drew out his pistol and took aim. . . . I counted the seconds. . . . I thought of her. . . . A terrible minute passed! Silvio lowered his hand.

"'I regret,' said he, 'that the pistol is not loaded with cherry- stones . . . the bullet is heavy. It seems to me that this is not a duel, but a murder. I am not accustomed to taking aim at unarmed men. Let us begin all over again; we will cast lots as to who shall fire first.'

"My head went round. . . . I think I raised some objection. . . . At last we loaded another pistol, and rolled up two pieces of paper. He placed these latter in his cap-- the same through which I had once sent a bullet--and again I drew the first number.

"'You are devilish lucky, Count,' said he, with a smile that I shall never forget.

"I don't know what was the matter with me, or how it was that he managed to make me do it . . . but I fired and hit that picture."

The Count pointed with his finger to the perforated picture; his face glowed like fire; the Countess was whiter than her own handkerchief; and I could not restrain an exclamation.

"I fired," continued the Count, "and, thank Heaven, missed my aim. Then Silvio . . . at that moment he was really terrible . . . Silvio raised his hand to take aim at me. Suddenly the door opens, Masha rushes into the room, and with a loud shriek throws herself upon my neck. Her presence restored to me all my courage.

"'My dear,' said I to her, 'don't you see that we are joking? How frightened you are! Go and drink a glass of water and then come back to us; I will introduce you to an old friend and comrade.'

"Masha still doubted.

"'Tell me, is my husband speaking the truth?' said she, turning to the terrible Silvio: 'is it true that you are only joking?'

"'He is always joking, Countess,' replied Silvio: 'once he gave me a slap in the face in a joke; on another occasion he sent a bullet through my cap in a joke; and just now, when he fired at me and missed me, it was all in a joke. And now I feel inclined for a joke.'

"With these words he raised his pistol to take aim at me--right before her! Masha threw herself at his feet.

"'Rise, Masha; are you not ashamed!' I cried in a rage: 'and you, sir, will you cease to make fun of a poor woman? Will you fire or not?'

"'I will not,' replied Silvio: 'I am satisfied. I have seen your confusion, your alarm. I forced you to fire at me. That is sufficient. You will remember me. I leave you to your conscience.'

"Then he turned to go, but pausing in the doorway, and looking at the picture that my shot had passed through, he fired at it almost without taking aim, and disappeared. My wife had fainted away; the servants did not venture to stop him, the mere look of him filled them with terror. He went out upon the steps, called his coachman, and drove off before I could recover myself."

The Count was silent. In this way I learned the end of the story, whose beginning had once made such a deep impression upon me. The hero of it I never saw again. It is said that Silvio commanded a detachment of Hetairists during the revolt under Alexander Ipsilanti, and that he was killed in the battle of Skoulana.

ST. JOHN'S EVE
BY
NIKOLAI VASILIEVITCH GOGOL

From "St. John's Eve." Translated by Isabel F. Hapgood.
1886
(RELATED BY THE SACRISTAN OF THE DIKANKA CHURCH)[3]

Thoma Grigorovitch had a very strange sort of eccentricity: to the day of his death he never liked to tell the same thing twice. There were times when, if you asked him to relate a thing afresh, behold, he would interpolate new matter, or alter it so that it was impossible to recognize it. Once on a time, one of those gentlemen (it is hard for us simple people to put a name to them, to say whether they are scribblers or not scribblers: but it is just the same thing as the usurers at our yearly fairs; they clutch and beg and steal every sort of frippery, and issue mean little volumes, no thicker than an ABC book, every month, or even every week),--one of these gentlemen wormed this same story out of Thoma Grigorovitch, and he completely forgot about it. But that same young gentleman in the pea-green caftan, whom I have mentioned, and one of whose Tales you have already read, I think, came from Poltava, bringing with him a little book, and, opening it in the middle, shows it to us. Thoma Grigorovitch was on the point of setting his spectacles astride of his nose, but recollected that he had forgotten to wind thread about them, and stick them together with wax, so he passed it over to me. As I understand something about reading and writing, and do not wear spectacles, I undertook to read it. I had not turned two leaves, when all at once he caught me

3   This is one of the stories from the celebrated volume entitled "Tales at a Farmhouse near Dikanka."

by the hand, and stopped me.

"Stop! tell me first what you are reading."

I confess that I was a trifle stunned by such a question.

"What! what am I reading, Thoma Grigorovitch? These were your very words."

"Who told you that they were my words?"

"Why, what more would you have? Here it is printed: RELATED BY SUCH AND SUCH A SACRISTAN."

"Spit on the head of the man who printed that! he lies, the dog of a Moscow pedler! Did I say that? 'TWAS JUST THE SAME AS THOUGH ONE HADN'T HIS WITS ABOUT HIM. Listen. I'll tell it to you on the spot."

We moved up to the table, and he began.

$$* \qquad * \qquad * \qquad *$$

My grandfather (the kingdom of heaven be his! may he eat only wheaten rolls and makovniki[4] with honey in the other world!) could tell a story wonderfully well. When he used to begin on a tale, you wouldn't stir from the spot all day, but keep on listening. He was no match for the story-teller of the present day, when he begins to lie, with a tongue as though he had had nothing to eat for three days, so that you snatch your cap and flee from the house. As I now recall it,--my old mother was alive then,--in the long winter evenings when the frost was crackling out of doors, and had so sealed up hermetically the narrow panes of our cottage, she used to sit before the hackling-comb, drawing out a long thread in her hand, rocking the cradle with her foot, and humming a song, which I seem to hear even now.

The fat-lamp, quivering and flaring up as though in fear of something, lighted us within our cottage; the spindle hummed; and all of us children, collected in a cluster, listened to grandfather, who had not crawled off the oven for more than five years, owing to his great age. But the wondrous tales of the incursions of the Zaporozhian Cossacks, the Poles, the bold deeds of Podkova, of Poltor-Kozhukh, and Sagaidatchnii, did not interest us so much as the stories about some deed of old which always sent a shiver through our frames, and made our hair rise upright on our heads. Sometimes such terror took possession of us in consequence of them,

---

4   Poppy-seeds cooked in honey, and dried in square cakes.

that, from that evening on, Heaven knows what a marvel everything seemed to us. If you chance to go out of the cottage after nightfall for anything, you imagine that a visitor from the other world has lain down to sleep in your bed; and I should not be able to tell this a second time were it not that I had often taken my own smock, at a distance, as it lay at the head of the bed, for the Evil One rolled up in a ball! But the chief thing about grandfather's stories was, that he never had lied in all his life; and whatever he said was so, was so.

I will now relate to you one of his marvellous tales. I know that there are a great many wise people who copy in the courts, and can even read civil documents, who, if you were to put into their hand a simple prayer-book, could not make out the first letter in it, and would show all their teeth in derision--which is wisdom. These people laugh at everything you tell them. Such incredulity has spread abroad in the world! What then? (Why, may God and the Holy Virgin cease to love me if it is not possible that even you will not believe me!) Once he said something about witches; . . . What then? Along comes one of these head- breakers,--and doesn't believe in witches! Yes, glory to God that I have lived so long in the world! I have seen heretics, to whom it would be easier to lie in confession than it would to our brothers and equals to take snuff, and those people would deny the existence of witches! But let them just dream about something, and they won't even tell what it was! There's no use in talking about them!

$$*\qquad*\qquad*\qquad*$$

ST. JOHN'S EVE.

No one could have recognized this village of ours a little over a hundred years ago: a hamlet it was, the poorest kind of a hamlet. Half a score of miserable izbas, unplastered, badly thatched, were scattered here and there about the fields. There was not an inclosure or decent shed to shelter animals or wagons. That was the way the wealthy lived; and if you had looked for our brothers, the poor,--why, a hole in the ground,--that was a cabin for you! Only by the smoke could you tell that a God-created man lived there. You ask why they lived so? It was not entirely through poverty: almost every one led a wandering, Cossack life, and gathered not a little plunder in foreign lands; it was rather because there was no reason for setting up a well-ordered khata (wooden house). How many people were wandering all over the country,--Crimeans, Poles, Lithuanians! It was quite possible that their own countrymen might make a descent, and plunder everything. Anything was possible.

In this hamlet a man, or rather a devil in human form, often made his appearance. Why he came, and whence, no one knew. He prowled about, got drunk, and suddenly disappeared as if into the air, and there was not a hint of his existence. Then, again, behold, he seemed to have dropped from the sky, and went flying about the streets of the village, of which no trace now remains, and which was not more than a hundred paces from Dikanka. He would collect together all the Cossacks he met; then there were songs, laughter, money in abundance, and vodka flowed like water. . . . He would address the pretty girls, and give them ribbons, earrings, strings of beads,--more than they knew what to do with. It is true that the pretty girls rather hesitated about accepting his presents: God knows, perhaps they had passed through unclean hands. My grandfather's aunt, who kept a tavern at that time, in which Basavriuk (as they called that devil-man) often had his carouses, said that no consideration on the face of the earth would have induced her to accept a gift from him. And then, again, how avoid accepting? Fear seized on every one when he knit his bristly brows, and gave a sidelong glance which might send your feet, God knows whither; but if you accept, then the next night some fiend from the swamp, with horns on his head, comes to call, and begins to squeeze your neck, when there is a string of beads upon it; or bite your finger, if there is a ring upon it; or drag you by the hair, if ribbons are braided in it. God have mercy, then, on those who owned such gifts! But here was the difficulty: it was impossible to get rid of them; if you threw them into the water, the diabolical ring or necklace would skim along the surface, and into your hand.

There was a church in the village,--St. Pantelei, if I remember rightly. There lived there a priest, Father Athanasii of blessed memory. Observing that Basavriuk did not come to church, even on Easter, he determined to reprove him, and impose penance upon him. Well, he hardly escaped with his life. "Hark ye, pannotche!"

[5] he thundered in reply, "learn to mind your own business instead of meddling in other people's, if you don't want that goat's throat of yours stuck together with boiling kutya."[6] What was to be done with this unrepentant man? Father Athanasii contented himself with announcing that any one who should make the acquaintance of Basavriuk would be counted a Catholic, an enemy of Christ's church, not a member of the human race.

In this village there was a Cossack named Korzh, who had a laborer whom people called Peter the Orphan--perhaps because no one remembered either his father or mother. The church starost, it is true, said that they had died of the pest in his second year; but my grandfather's aunt would not hear to that, and tried with all her might to furnish him with parents, although poor Peter needed them about as much as we need last year's snow. She said that his father had been in Zaporozhe, taken prisoner by the Turks, underwent God only knows what tortures, and having, by some miracle, disguised himself as a eunuch, had made his escape. Little cared the black-browed youths and maidens about his parents. They merely remarked, that if he only had a new coat, a red sash, a black lambskin cap, with dandified blue crown, on his head, a Turkish sabre hanging by his side, a whip in one hand and a pipe with handsome mountings in the other, he would surpass all the young men. But the pity was, that the only thing poor Peter had was a gray svitka with more holes in it than there are gold-pieces in a Jew's pocket. And that was not the worst of it, but this: that Korzh had a daughter, such a beauty as I think you can hardly have chanced to see. My deceased grandfather's aunt used to say--and you know that it is easier for a woman to kiss the Evil One than to call anybody a beauty, without malice be it said--that this Cossack maiden's cheeks were as plump and fresh as the pinkest poppy when just bathed in God's dew, and, glowing, it unfolds its petals, and coquets with the rising sun; that her brows were like black cords, such as our maidens buy nowadays, for their crosses and ducats, of the Moscow pedlers who visit the villages with their baskets, and evenly arched as though peeping into her clear eyes; that her little mouth, at sight of which the youths smacked their lips, seemed made to emit the songs of nightingales; that her hair, black as the raven's wing, and soft as young flax (our maidens did not then plait their hair in clubs

5 Sir
6 A dish of rice or wheat flour, with honey and raisins, which is brought to the church on the celebration of memorial masses

interwoven with pretty, bright-hued ribbons) fell in curls over her kuntush.[7] Eh! may I never intone another alleluia in the choir, if I would not have kissed her, in spite of the gray which is making its way all through the old wool which covers my pate, and my old woman beside me, like a thorn in my side! Well, you know what happens when young men and maids live side by side. In the twilight the heels of red boots were always visible in the place where Pidorka chatted with her Petrus. But Korzh would never have suspected anything out of the way, only one day--it is evident that none but the Evil One could have inspired him--Petrus took it into his head to kiss the Cossack maiden's rosy lips with all his heart in the passage, without first looking well about him; and that same Evil One-- may the son of a dog dream of the holy cross!--caused the old graybeard, like a fool, to open the cottage-door at that same moment. Korzh was petrified, dropped his jaw, and clutched at the door for support. Those unlucky kisses had completely stunned him. It surprised him more than the blow of a pestle on the wall, with which, in our days, the muzhik generally drives out his intoxication for lack of fuses and powder.

Recovering himself, he took his grandfather's hunting-whip from the wall, and was about to belabor Peter's back with it, when Pidorka's little six-year-old brother Ivas rushed up from somewhere or other, and, grasping his father's legs with his little hands, screamed out, "Daddy, daddy! don't beat Petrus!" What was to be done? A father's heart is not made of stone. Hanging the whip again upon the wall, he led him quietly from the house. "If you ever show yourself in my cottage again, or even under the windows, look out, Petro! by Heaven, your black moustache will disappear; and your black locks, though wound twice about your ears, will take leave of your pate, or my name is not Terentiy Korzh." So saying, he gave him a little taste of his fist in the nape of his neck, so that all grew dark before Petrus, and he flew headlong. So there was an end of their kissing. Sorrow seized upon our doves; and a rumor was rife in the village, that a certain Pole, all embroidered with gold, with moustaches, sabres, spurs, and pockets jingling like the bells of the bag with which our sacristan Taras goes through the church every day, had begun to frequent Korzh's house. Now, it is well known why the father is visited when there is a black-browed daughter about. So, one day, Pidorka burst into tears, and clutched the hand of her Ivas. "Ivas, my dear! Ivas, my love! fly to Petrus, my child

---

7   Upper garment in Little Russia.

of gold, like an arrow from a bow. Tell him all: I would have loved his brown eyes, I would have kissed his white face, but my fate decrees not so. More than one towel have I wet with burning tears. I am sad, I am heavy at heart. And my own father is my enemy. I will not marry that Pole, whom I do not love. Tell him they are pre-paring a wedding, but there will be no music at our wedding: ecclesiastics will sing instead of pipes and kobzas.[8] I shall not dance with my bridegroom: they will carry me out. Dark, dark will be my dwelling,--of maple wood; and, instead of chimneys, a cross will stand upon the roof."

Petro stood petrified, without moving from the spot, when the innocent child lisped out Pidorka's words to him. "And I, unhappy man, thought to go to the Crimea and Turkey, win gold and return to thee, my beauty! But it may not be. The evil eye has seen us. I will have a wedding, too, dear little fish, I too; but no ecclesiastics will be at that wedding. The black crow will caw, instead of the pope, over me; the smooth field will be my dwelling; the dark blue clouds my roof-tree. The eagle will claw out my brown eyes: the rain will wash the Cossack's bones, and the whirlwinds will dry them. But what am I? Of whom, to whom, am I com-plaining? 'T is plain, God willed it so. If I am to be lost, then so be it!" and he went straight to the tavern.

My late grandfather's aunt was somewhat surprised on seeing Petrus in the tavern, and at an hour when good men go to morning mass; and she stared at him as though in a dream, when he demanded a jug of brandy, about half a pailful. But the poor fellow tried in vain to drown his woe. The vodka stung his tongue like net-tles, and tasted more bitter than wormwood. He flung the jug from him upon the ground. "You have sorrowed enough, Cossack," growled a bass voice behind him. He looked round--Basavriuk! Ugh, what a face! His hair was like a brush, his eyes like those of a bull. "I know what you lack: here it is." Then he jingled a leather purse which hung from his girdle, and smiled diabolically. Petro shuddered. "He, he, he! yes, how it shines!" he roared, shaking out ducats into his hand: "he, he, he! and how it jingles! And I only ask one thing for a whole pile of such shiners."-- "It is the Evil One!" exclaimed Petro: "Give them here! I'm ready for anything!" They struck hands upon it. "See here, Petro, you are ripe just in time: to-morrow is St. John the Baptist's day. Only on this one night in the year does the fern blossom.

---

8   Eight-stringed musical instrument.

Delay not. I will await thee at midnight in the Bear's ravine."

I do not believe that chickens await the hour when the woman brings their corn with as much anxiety as Petrus awaited the evening. And, in fact, he looked to see whether the shadows of the trees were not lengthening, if the sun were not turning red towards setting; and the longer he watched, the more impatient he grew. How long it was! Evidently, God's day had lost its end somewhere. And now the sun is gone. The sky is red only on one side, and it is already growing dark. It grows colder in the fields. It gets dusky and more dusky, and at last quite dark. At last! With heart almost bursting from his bosom, he set out on his way, and cautiously descended through the dense woods into the deep hollow called the Bear's ravine. Basavriuk was already waiting there. It was so dark, that you could not see a yard before you. Hand in hand they penetrated the thin marsh, clinging to the luxuriant thorn bushes, and stumbling at almost every step. At last they reached an open spot. Petro looked about him: he had never chanced to come there before. Here Basavriuk halted.

"Do you see, before you stand three hillocks? There are a great many sorts of flowers upon them. But may some power keep you from plucking even one of them. But as soon as the fern blossoms, seize it, and look not round, no matter what may seem to be going on behind thee."

Petro wanted to ask--and behold he was no longer there. He approached the three hillocks--where were the flowers? He saw nothing. The wild steppe-grass darkled around, and stifled everything in its luxuriance. But the lightning flashed; and before him stood a whole bed of flowers, all wonderful, all strange: and there were also the simple fronds of fern. Petro doubted his senses, and stood thoughtfully before them, with both hands upon his sides.

"What prodigy is this? one can see these weeds ten times in a day: what marvel is there about them? was not devil's-face laughing at me?"

Behold! the tiny flower-bud crimsons, and moves as though alive. It is a marvel, in truth. It moves, and grows larger and larger, and flushes like a burning coal. The tiny star flashes up, something bursts softly, and the flower opens before his eyes like a flame, lighting the others about it. "Now is the time," thought Petro, and extended his hand. He sees hundreds of shaggy hands reach from behind him, also for the flower; and there is a running about from place to place, in the rear. He half shut his eyes, plucked sharply at the stalk, and the flower remained in his hand. All became still. Upon a stump sat Basavriuk, all blue like a corpse. He moved not so much as a finger. His eyes were immovably fixed on something visible to him alone: his mouth was half open and speechless. All about, nothing stirred. Ugh! it was horrible!-- But then a whistle was heard, which made Petro's heart grow cold within him; and it seemed to him that the grass whispered, and the flowers began to talk among themselves in delicate voices, like little silver bells; the trees rustled in waving contention;--Basavriuk's face suddenly became full of life, and his eyes sparkled. "The witch has just returned," he muttered between his teeth. "See here, Petro: a beauty will stand before you in a moment; do whatever she commands; if not--you are lost for ever." Then he parted the thorn-bush with a knotty stick, and before him stood a tiny izba, on chicken's legs, as they say. Basavriuk smote it with his fist, and the wall trembled. A large black dog ran out to meet them, and with a whine, transforming itself into a cat, flew straight at his eyes. "Don't be angry, don't be angry, you old Satan!" said Basavriuk, employing such words as would have made a good man stop his ears. Behold, instead of a cat, an old woman with a face wrinkled like a baked apple, and all bent into a bow: her nose and chin were like a pair of nut-crackers. "A stunning beauty!" thought Petro; and cold chills ran down his back. The witch tore the flower from his hand, bent over, and muttered over it for a long time, sprinkling it with some kind of water. Sparks flew from her mouth, froth appeared on her lips.

"Throw it away," she said, giving it back to Petro.

Petro threw it, and what wonder was this? the flower did not fall straight to the earth, but for a long while twinkled like a fiery ball through the darkness, and swam through the air like a boat: at last it began to sink lower and lower, and fell so far away, that the little star, hardly larger than a poppy-seed, was barely visible. "Here!" croaked the old woman, in a dull voice: and Basavriuk, giving him a spade, said: "Dig here, Petro: here you will see more gold than you or Korzh ever dreamed of."

Petro spat on his hands, seized the spade, applied his foot, and turned up the earth, a second, a third, a fourth time. . . . There was something hard: the spade clinked, and would go no farther. Then his eyes began to distinguish a small, iron-bound coffer. He tried to seize it; but the chest began to sink into the earth, deeper, farther, and deeper still: and behind him he heard a laugh, more like a serpent's hiss. "No, you shall not see the gold until you procure human blood," said the witch, and led up to him a child of six, covered with a white sheet, indicating by a sign that he was to cut off his head. Petro was stunned. A trifle, indeed, to cut off a man's, or even an innocent child's, head for no reason whatever! In wrath he tore off the sheet enveloping his head, and behold! before him stood Ivas. And the poor child crossed his little hands, and hung his head. . . . Petro flew upon the witch with the knife like a madman, and was on the point of laying hands on her. . . .

"What did you promise for the girl?" . . . thundered Basavriuk; and like a shot he was on his back. The witch stamped her foot: a blue flame flashed from the earth; it illumined it all inside, and it was as if moulded of crystal; and all that was within the earth became visible, as if in the palm of the hand. Ducats, precious stones in chests and kettles, were piled in heaps beneath the very spot they stood on. His eyes burned, . . . his mind grew troubled. . . . He grasped the knife like a madman, and the innocent blood spurted into his eyes. Diabolical laughter resounded on all sides. Misshaped monsters flew past him in herds. The witch, fastening her hands in the headless trunk, like a wolf drank its blood. . . . All went round in his head. Collecting all his strength, he set out to run. Everything turned red before him. The trees seemed steeped in blood, and burned and groaned. The sky glowed and glowered. . . . Burning points, like lightning, flickered before his eyes. Utterly exhausted, he rushed into his miserable hovel, and fell to the ground like a log. A death-like sleep overpowered him.

Two days and two nights did Petro sleep, without once awakening. When he came to himself, on the third day, he looked long at all the corners of his hut; but in vain did he endeavor to recollect; his memory was like a miser's pocket, from which you cannot entice a quarter of a kopek. Stretching himself, he heard something clash at his feet. He looked, . . . two bags of gold. Then only, as if in a dream, he recollected that he had been seeking some treasure, that something had frightened him in the woods. . . . But at what price he had obtained it, and how, he could by no means understand.

Korzh saw the sacks,--and was mollified. "Such a Petrus, quite unheard of! yes, and did I not love him? Was he not to me as my own son?" And the old fellow carried on his fiction until it reduced him to tears. Pidorka began to tell him how some passing gypsies had stolen Ivas; but Petro could not even recall him--to such a degree had the Devil's influence darkened his mind! There was no reason for delay. The Pole was dismissed, and the wedding-feast prepared; rolls were baked, towels and handkerchiefs embroidered; the young people were seated at table; the wedding-loaf was cut; banduras, cymbals, pipes, kobzi, sounded, and pleasure was rife . . .

A wedding in the olden times was not like one of the present day. My grand-father's aunt used to tell--what doings!--how the maidens--in festive head-dresses of yellow, blue, and pink ribbons, above which they bound gold braid; in thin chemisettes embroidered on all the seams with red silk, and strewn with tiny silver flowers; in morocco shoes, with high iron heels--danced the gorlitza as swimmingly as peacocks, and as wildly as the whirlwind; how the youths--with their ship-shaped caps upon their heads, the crowns of gold brocade, with a little slit at the nape where the hair-net peeped through, and two horns projecting, one in front and another behind, of the very finest black lambskin; in kuntushas of the finest blue silk with red borders--stepped forward one by one, their arms akimbo in state-ly form, and executed the gopak; how the lads--in tall Cossack caps, and light cloth svitkas, girt with silver embroidered belts, their short pipes in their teeth--skipped before them, and talked nonsense. Even Korzh could not contain himself, as he gazed at the young people, from getting gay in his old age. Bandura in hand, alter-nately puffing at his pipe and singing, a brandy- glass upon his head, the gray-beard began the national dance amid loud shouts from the merry-makers. What will not people devise in merry mood! They even began to disguise their faces. They did not look like human beings. They are not to be compared with the disguises which we have at our weddings nowadays. What do they do now? Why, imitate gypsies and Moscow pedlers. No! then one used to dress himself as a Jew, another as the Devil: they would begin by kissing each other, and ended by seizing each other by the hair. . . . God be with them! you laughed till you held your sides. They dressed themselves in Turkish and Tartar garments. All upon them glowed like a conflagra-tion, . . . and then they began to joke and play pranks. . . . Well, then away with the saints! An amusing thing happened to my grandfather's aunt, who was at this wed-ding. She was dressed in a voluminous Tartar robe, and, wine-glass in hand, was entertaining the company. The Evil One instigated one man to pour vodka over her from behind. Another, at the same moment, evidently not by accident, struck a light, and touched it to her; . . . the flame flashed up; poor aunt, in terror, flung her robe from her, before them all. . . . Screams, laughter, jest, arose, as if at a fair. In a word, the old folks could not recall so merry a wedding.

Pidorka and Petrus began to live like a gentleman and lady. There was plenty of everything, and everything was handsome. . . . But honest people shook their heads when they looked at their way of living. "From the Devil no good can come," they unanimously agreed. "Whence, except from the tempter of orthodox people, came this wealth? Where else could he get such a lot of gold? Why, on the very day that he got rich, did Basavriuk vanish as if into thin air?" Say, if you can, that people imagine things! In fact, a month had not passed, and no one would have recognized Petrus. Why, what had happened to him? God knows. He sits in one spot, and says no word to any one: he thinks continually, and seems to be trying to recall something. When Pidorka succeeds in getting him to speak, he seems to forget himself, carries on a conversation, and even grows cheerful; but if he inadvertently glances at the sacks, "Stop, stop! I have forgotten," he cries, and again plunges into reverie, and again strives to recall something. Sometimes when he has sat long in a place, it seems to him as though it were coming, just coming back to mind, . . . and again all fades away. It seems as if he is sitting in the tavern: they bring him vodka; vodka stings him; vodka is repulsive to him. Some one comes along, and strikes him on the shoulder; . . . but beyond that everything is veiled in darkness before him. The perspiration streams down his face, and he sits exhausted in the same place.

What did not Pidorka do? She consulted the sorceress; and they poured out fear, and brewed stomach ache,[9]--but all to no avail. And so the summer passed. Many a Cossack had mowed and reaped: many a Cossack, more enterprising than the rest, had set off upon an expedition. Flocks of ducks were already crowding our marshes, but there was not even a hint of improvement.

It was red upon the steppes. Ricks of grain, like Cossacks' caps, dotted the

---

9 "To pour out fear," is done with us in case of fear; when it is desired to know what caused it, melted lead or wax is poured into water, and the object whose form it assumes is the one which frightened the sick person; after this, the fear departs. Sonyashnitza is brewed for giddiness, and pain in the bowels. To this end, a bit of stump is burned, thrown into a jug, and turned upside down into a bowl filled with water, which is placed on the patient's stomach: after an incantation, he is given a spoonful of this water to drink.

fields here and there. On the highway were to be encountered wagons loaded with brushwood and logs. The ground had become more solid, and in places was touched with frost. Already had the snow begun to besprinkle the sky, and the branches of the trees were covered with rime like rabbit-skin. Already on frosty days the red-breasted finch hopped about on the snow-heaps like a foppish Polish nobleman, and picked out grains of corn; and children, with huge sticks, chased wooden tops upon the ice; while their fathers lay quietly on the stove, issuing forth at intervals with lighted pipes in their lips, to growl, in regular fashion, at the ortho-dox frost, or to take the air, and thresh the grain spread out in the barn. At last the snow began to melt, and the ice rind slipped away: but Petro remained the same; and, the longer it went on, the more morose he grew. He sat in the middle of the cottage as though nailed to the spot, with the sacks of gold at his feet. He grew shy, his hair grew long, he became terrible; and still he thought of but one thing, still he tried to recall something, and got angry and ill- tempered because he could not recall it. Often, rising wildly from his seat, he gesticulates violently, fixes his eyes on something as though desirous of catching it: his lips move as though desirous of uttering some long-forgotten word--and remain speechless. Fury takes possession of him: he gnaws and bites his hands like a man half crazy, and in his vexation tears out his hair by the handful, until, calming down, he falls into forgetfulness, as it were, and again begins to recall, and is again seized with fury and fresh tortures. . . . What visitation of God is this?

Pidorka was neither dead nor alive. At first it was horrible to her to remain alone in the cottage; but, in course of time, the poor woman grew accustomed to her sorrow. But it was impossible to recognize the Pidorka of former days. No blush, no smile: she was thin and worn with grief, and had wept her bright eyes away. Once, some one who evidently took pity on her advised her to go to the witch who dwelt in the Bear's ravine, and enjoyed the reputation of being able to cure every disease in the world. She determined to try this last remedy: word by word she persuaded the old woman to come to her. This was St. John's Eve, as it chanced. Petro lay in-sensible on the bench, and did not observe the new- comer. Little by little he rose, and looked about him. Suddenly he trembled in every limb, as though he were on the scaffold: his hair rose upon his head, . . . and he laughed such a laugh as pierced Pidorka's heart with fear. "I have remembered, remembered!" he cried in terrible joy; and, swinging a hatchet round his head, he flung it at the old woman with all his might. The hatchet penetrated the oaken door two vershok (three inches and a half). The old woman disappeared; and a child of seven in a white blouse, with covered head, stood in the middle of the cottage. . . . The sheet flew off. "Ivas!" cried Pidorka, and ran to him; but the apparition became covered from head to foot with blood, and illumined the whole room with red light. . . . She ran into the passage in her terror, but, on recovering herself a little, wished to help him; in vain! the door had slammed to behind her so securely that she could not open it. People ran up, and began to knock: they broke in the door, as though there was but one mind among them. The whole cottage was full of smoke; and just in the middle, where Petrus had stood, was a heap of ashes, from which smoke was still rising. They flung themselves upon the sacks: only broken potsherds lay there instead of ducats. The Cossacks stood with staring eyes and open mouths, not daring to move a hair, as if rooted to the earth, such terror did this wonder inspire in them.

I do not remember what happened next. Pidorka took a vow to go upon a pilgrimage, collected the property left her by her father, and in a few days it was as if she had never been in the village. Whither she had gone, no one could tell. Officious old women would have despatched her to the same place whither Petro had gone; but a Cossack from Kief reported that he had seen in a cloister, a nun withered to a mere skeleton, who prayed unceasingly; and her fellow villagers recognized her as Pidorka, by all the signs,--that no one had ever heard her utter a word; that she had come on foot, and had brought a frame for the ikon of God's mother, set with such brilliant stones that all were dazzled at the sight.

But this was not the end, if you please. On the same day that the Evil One made way with Petrus, Basavriuk appeared again; but all fled from him. They knew what sort of a bird he was,--none else than Satan, who had assumed human form in order to unearth treasures; and, since treasures do not yield to unclean hands, he seduced the young. That same year, all deserted their earth huts, and collected in a village; but, even there, there was no peace, on account of that accursed Basavriuk. My late grandfather's aunt said that he was particularly angry with her, because she had abandoned her former tavern, and tried with all his might to revenge himself upon her. Once the village elders were assembled in the tavern, and, as the saying goes, were arranging the precedence at the table, in the middle of which was placed a small roasted lamb, shame to say. They chattered about this, that, and the other,--among the rest about various marvels and strange things. Well, they saw something; it would have been nothing if only one had seen it, but all saw it; and it was this: the sheep raised his head; his goggling eyes became alive and sparkled; and the black, bristling moustache, which appeared for one instant, made a significant gesture at those present. All, at once, recognized Basavriuk's countenance in the sheep's head: my grandfather's aunt thought it was on the point of asking for vodka. ... The worthy elders seized their hats, and hastened home.

Another time, the church starost[10] himself, who was fond of an occasional private interview with my grandfather's brandy- glass, had not succeeded in getting to the bottom twice, when he beheld the glass bowing very low to him. "Satan take you, let us make the sign of the cross over you!" ... And the same marvel happened to his better- half. She had just begun to mix the dough in a huge kneading-trough, when suddenly the trough sprang up. "Stop, stop! where are you going?" Putting its arms akimbo, with dignity, it went skipping all about the cottage. ... You may laugh, but it was no laughing-matter to our grandfathers. And in vain did Father Athanasii go through all the village with holy water, and chase the Devil through all the streets with his brush; and my late grandfather's aunt long complained that, as soon as it was dark, some one came knocking at her door, and scratching at the wall.

Well! All appears to be quiet now, in the place where our village stands; but it was not so very long ago--my father was still alive--that I remember how a good man could not pass the ruined tavern, which a dishonest race had long managed for their own interest. From the smoke- blackened chimneys, smoke poured out in a pillar, and rising high in the air, as if to take an observation, rolled off like a cap, scattering burning coals over the steppe; and Satan (the son of a dog should not be mentioned) sobbed so pitifully in his lair, that the startled ravens rose in flocks from the neighboring oak-wood, and flew through the air with wild cries.

---

10   Elder

AN OLD ACQUAINTANCE
BY
COUNT LYOF N. TOLSTOI

From "The Invaders." Translated by N. H. Dole.
1887

(Prince Nekhiludof Relates how, during an Expedition in the Caucasus, he met an Acquaintance from Moscow)

Our division had been out in the field. The work in hand was accomplished: we had cut a way through the forest, and each day we were expecting from headquarters orders for our return to the fort. Our division of fieldpieces was stationed at the top of a steep mountain- crest which was terminated by the swift mountain-river Mechik, and had to command the plain that stretched before us. Here and there on this picturesque plain, out of the reach of gunshot, now and then, especially at evening, groups of mounted mountaineers showed themselves, attracted by curiosity to ride up and view the Russian camp.

The evening was clear, mild, and fresh, as it is apt to be in December in the Caucasus; the sun was setting behind the steep chain of the mountains at the left, and threw rosy rays upon the tents scattered over the slope, upon the soldiers moving about, and upon our two guns, which seemed to crane their necks as they rested motionless on the earthwork two paces from us. The infantry picket, stationed on the knoll at the left, stood in perfect silhouette against the light of the sunset; no less distinct were the stacks of muskets, the form of the sentry, the groups of soldiers, and the smoke of the smouldering camp-fire.

At the right and left of the slope, on the black, sodden earth, the tents gleamed white; and behind the tents, black, stood the bare trunks of the platane forest, which rang with the incessant sound of axes, the crackling of the bonfires, and the crashing of the trees as they fell under the axes. The bluish smoke arose from tobacco-pipes on all sides, and vanished in the transparent blue of the frosty sky. By the tents and on the lower ground around the arms rushed the Cossacks, dragoons, and artillerists, with great galloping and snorting of horses as they returned from getting water. It began to freeze; all sounds were heard with extraordinary distinctness, and one could see an immense distance across the plain through the clear, rare atmosphere. The groups of the enemy, their curiosity at seeing the soldiers satisfied, quietly galloped off across the fields, still yellow with the golden corn- stubble, toward their auls, or villages, which were visible beyond the forest, with the tall posts of the cemeteries and the smoke rising in the air.

Our tent was pitched not far from the guns on a place high and dry, from which we had a remarkably extended view. Near the tent, on a cleared space, around the battery itself, we had our games of skittles, or chushki. The obliging soldiers had made for us rustic benches and tables. On account of all these amusements, the artillery officers, our comrades, and a few infantry men liked to gather of an evening around our battery, and the place came to be called the club.

As the evening was fine, the best players had come, and we were amusing ourselves with skittles[11]. Ensign D., Lieutenant O., and myself had played two games in succession; and to the common satisfaction and amusement of all the spectators, officers, soldiers, and servants[12] who were watching us from their tents, we had twice carried the winning party on our backs from one end of the ground to the other. Especially droll was the situation of the huge fat Captain S., who, puffing and smiling good-naturedly, with legs dragging on the ground, rode pickaback on the feeble little Lieutenant O.

When it grew somewhat later, the servants brought three glasses of tea for the six men of us, and not a spoon; and we who had finished our game came to the plaited settees.

There was standing near them a small bow-legged man, a stranger to us, in a sheepskin jacket, and a papakha, or Circassian cap, with a long overhanging white

11   Gorodki
12   Denshchiki

crown. As soon as we came near where he stood, he took a few irresolute steps, and put on his cap; and several times he seemed to make up his mind to come to meet us, and then stopped again. But after deciding, probably, that it was impossible to remain irresolute, the stranger took off his cap, and, going in a circuit around us, approached Captain S.

"Ah, Guskantinli, how is it, old man?"[13] said S., still smiling good-naturedly, under the influence of his ride.

Guskantni, as S. called him, instantly replaced his cap, and made a motion as though to thrust his hands into the pockets of his jacket;[14] but on the side toward me there was no pocket in the jacket, and his small red hand fell into an awkward position. I felt a strong desire to make out who this man was (was he a yunker, or a degraded officer?), and, not realizing that my gaze (that is, the gaze of a strange officer) disconcerted him, I continued to stare at his dress and appearance.

I judged that he was about thirty. His small, round, gray eyes had a sleepy expression, and at the same time gazed calmly out from under the dirty white lamb-skin of his cap, which hung down over his face. His thick, irregular nose, standing out between his sunken cheeks, gave evidence of emaciation that was the result of illness, and not natural. His restless lips, barely covered by a sparse, soft, whitish moustache, were constantly changing their shape as though they were trying to assume now one expression, now another. But all these expressions seemed to be endless, and his face retained one predominating expression of timidity and fright. Around his thin neck, where the veins stood out, was tied a green woollen scarf tucked into his jacket, his fur jacket, or polushubok, was worn bare, short, and had dog-fur sewed on the collar and on the false pockets. The trousers were checkered, of ash-gray color, and his sapogi had short, unblacked military bootlegs.

"I beg of you, do not disturb yourself," said I when he for the second time, tim-idly glancing at me, had taken off his cap.

He bowed to me with an expression of gratitude, replaced his hat, and, drawing from his pocket a dirty chintz tobacco-pouch with lacings, began to roll a cigarette.

I myself had not been long a yunker, an elderly yunker; and as I was incapable, as yet, of being good-naturedly serviceable to my younger comrades, and without means, I well knew all the moral difficulties of this situation for a proud man no

13   Nu chto, batenka
14   Polushubok, little half shuba, or fur cloak.

longer young, and I sympathized with all men who found themselves in such a situation, and I endeavored to make clear to myself their character and rank, and the tendencies of their intellectual peculiarities, in order to judge of the degree of their moral sufferings. This yunker or degraded officer, judging by his restless eyes and that intentionally constant variation of expression which I noticed in him, was a man very far from stupid, and extremely egotistical, and therefore much to be pitied.

Captain S. invited us to play another game of skittles, with the stakes to consist, not only of the usual pickaback ride of the winning party, but also of a few bottles of red wine, rum, sugar, cinnamon, and cloves for the mulled wine which that winter, on account of the cold, was greatly popular in our division.

Guskantini, as S. again called him, was also invited to take part; but before the game began, the man, struggling between gratification because he had been invited and a certain timidity, drew Captain S. aside, and began to say something in a whisper. The good-natured captain punched him in the ribs with his big, fat hand, and replied, loud enough to be heard:

"Not at all, old fellow[15], I assure you."

When the game was over, and that side in which the stranger whose rank was so low had taken part, had come out winners, and it fell to his lot to ride on one of our officers, Ensign D., the ensign grew red in the face: he went to the little divan and offered the stranger a cigarette by way of a compromise.

While they were ordering the mulled wine, and in the steward's tent were heard assiduous preparations on the part of Nikita, who had sent an orderly for cinnamon and cloves, and the shadow of his back was alternately lengthening and shortening on the dingy sides of the tent, we men, seven in all, sat around on the benches; and while we took turns in drinking tea from the three glasses, and gazed out over the plain, which was now beginning to glow in the twilight, we talked and laughed over the various incidents of the game.

The stranger in the fur jacket took no share in the conversation, obstinately refused to drink the tea which I several times offered him, and as he sat there on the ground in Tartar fashion, occupied himself in making cigarettes of fine-cut tobacco, and smoking them one after another, evidently not so much for his own satisfac-

---

15   Batenka, Malo-Russian diminutive, little father

tion as to give himself the appearance of a man with something to do. When it was remarked that the summons to return was expected on the morrow, and that there might be an engagement, he lifted himself on his knees, and, addressing Captain B. only, said that he had been at the adjutant's, and had himself written the order for the return on the next day. We all said nothing while he was speaking; and notwithstanding the fact that he was so bashful, we begged him to repeat this most interesting piece of news. He repeated what he had said, adding only that he had been staying at the adjutant's (since he made it his home there) when the order came.

"Look here, old fellow, if you are not telling us false, I shall have to go to my company and give some orders for to-morrow," said Captain S.

"No . . . why . . . it may be, I am sure," . . . stammered the stranger, but suddenly stopped, and, apparently feeling himself affronted, contracted his brows, and, muttering something between his teeth, again began to roll a cigarette. But the fine-cut tobacco in his chintz pouch began to show signs of giving out, and he asked S. to lend him a little cigarette.[16]

We kept on for a considerable time with that monotonous military chatter which every one who has ever been on an expedition will appreciate; all of us, with one and the same expression, complaining of the dullness and length of the expedition, in one and the same fashion sitting in judgment on our superiors, and all of us likewise, as we had done many times before, praising one comrade, pitying another, wondering how much this one had gained, how much that one had lost, and so on, and so on.

"Here, fellows, this adjutant of ours is completely broken up," said Captain S. "At headquarters he was everlastingly on the winning side; no matter whom he sat down with, he'd rake in everything: but now for two months past he has been losing all the time. The present expedition hasn't been lucky for him. I think he has got away with two thousand silver rubles and five hundred rubles' worth of articles,--the carpet that he won at Mukhin's, Nikitin's pistols, Sada's gold watch which Vorontsof gave him. He has lost it all."

"The truth of the matter in his case," said Lieutenant O., "was that he used to cheat everybody; it was impossible to play with him."

---

16 PAPIROSTCHKA, diminished diminutive of PAPIROSKA, from PAPIROS.

"He cheated every one, but now it's all gone up in his pipe;" and here Captain S. laughed good-naturedly. "Our friend Guskof here lives with him. He hasn't quite lost HIM yet: that's so, isn't it, old fellow?"[17] he asked, addressing Guskof.

Guskof tried to laugh. It was a melancholy, sickly laugh, which completely changed the expression of his countenance. Till this moment it had seemed to me that I had seen and known this man before; and, besides the name Guskof, by which Captain S. called him, was familiar to me; but how and when I had seen and known him, I actually could not remember.

"Yes," said Guskof, incessantly putting his hand to his moustaches, but instantly dropping it again without touching them. "Pavel Dmitrievitch's luck has been against him in this expedition, such a veine de malheur" he added in a careful but pure French pronunciation, again giving me to think that I had seen him, and seen him often, somewhere. "I know Pavel Dmitrievitch very well. He has great confidence in me," he proceeded to say; "he and I are old friends; that is, he is fond of me," he explained, evidently fearing that it might be taken as presumption for him to claim old friendship with the adjutant. "Pavel Dmitrievitch plays admirably; but now, strange as it may seem, it's all up with him, he is just about perfectly ruined; la chance a tourne," he added, addressing himself particularly to me.

At first we had listened to Guskof with condescending attention; but as soon as he made use of that second French phrase, we all involuntarily turned from him.

"I have played with him a thousand times, and we agreed then that it was strange," said Lieutenant O., with peculiar emphasis on the word STRANGE[18]. "I never once won a ruble from him. Why was it, when I used to win of others?"

"Pavel Dmitrievitch plays admirably: I have known him for a long time," said I. In fact, I had known the adjutant for several years; more than once I had seen him in the full swing of a game, surrounded by officers, and I had remarked his handsome, rather gloomy and always passionless calm face, his deliberate Malo-Russian pronunciation, his handsome belongings and horses, his bold, manly figure, and above all his skill and self-restraint in carrying on the game accurately and agreeably. More than once, I am sorry to say, as I looked at his plump white hands with a diamond ring on the index-finger, passing out one card after another, I grew angry with that ring, with his white hands, with the whole of the adjutant's person, and

17 Batenka
18 Stranno

evil thoughts on his account arose in my mind. But as I afterwards reconsidered the matter coolly, I persuaded myself that he played more skilfully than all with whom he happened to play: the more so, because as I heard his general observations concerning the game,--how one ought not to back out when one had laid the smallest stake, how one ought not to leave off in certain cases as the first rule for honest men, and so forth, and so forth,--it was evident that he was always on the winning side merely from the fact that he played more sagaciously and coolly than the rest of us. And now it seemed that this self-reliant, careful player had been stripped not only of his money but of his effects, which marks the lowest depths of loss for an officer.

"He always had devilish good luck with me," said Lieutenant O. "I made a vow never to play with him again."

"What a marvel you are, old fellow!" said S., nodding at me, and addressing O. "You lost three hundred silver rubles, that's what you lost to him."

"More than that," said the lieutenant savagely.

"And now you have come to your senses; it is rather late in the day, old man, for the rest of us have known for a long time that he was the cheat of the regiment," said S., with difficulty restraining his laughter, and feeling very well satisfied with his fabrication. "Here is Guskof right here,--he FIXES his cards for him. That's the reason of the friendship between them, old man"[19] . . . and Captain S., shaking all over, burst out into such a hearty "ha, ha, ha!" that he spilt the glass of mulled wine which he was holding in his hand. On Guskof's pale emaciated face there showed something like a color; he opened his mouth several times, raised his hands to his moustaches, and once more dropped them to his side where the pockets should have been, stood up, and then sat down again, and finally in an unnatural voice said to S.:

"It's no joke, Nikolai Ivanovitch, for you to say such things before people who don't know me and who see me in this unlined jacket . . . because--" His voice failed him, and again his small red hands with their dirty nails went from his jacket to his face, touching his moustache, his hair, his nose, rubbing his eyes, or needlessly scratching his cheek.

"As to saying that, everybody knows it, old fellow," continued S., thoroughly

---

19 BATENKA MOI

satisfied with his jest, and not heeding Guskof's complaint. Guskof was still trying to say something; and placing the palm of his right hand on his left knee in a most unnatural position, and gazing at S., he had an appearance of smiling contemptuously.

"No," said I to myself, as I noticed that smile of his, "I have not only seen him, but have spoken with him somewhere."

"You and I have met somewhere," said I to him when, under the influence of the common silence, S.'s laughter began to calm down. Guskof's mobile face suddenly lighted up, and his eyes, for the first time with a truly joyous expression, rested upon me.

"Why, I recognized you immediately," he replied in French. "In '48 I had the pleasure of meeting you quite frequently in Moscow at my sister's."

I had to apologize for not recognizing him at first in that costume and in that new garb. He arose, came to me, and with his moist hand irresolutely and weakly seized my hand, and sat down by me. Instead of looking at me, though he apparently seemed so glad to see me, he gazed with an expression of unfriendly bravado at the officers.

Either because I recognized in him a man whom I had met a few years before in a dresscoat in a parlor, or because he was suddenly raised in his own opinion by the fact of being recognized,--at all events it seemed to me that his face and even his motions completely changed: they now expressed lively intelligence, a childish self-satisfaction in the consciousness of such intelligence, and a certain contemptuous indifference; so that I confess, notwithstanding the pitiable position in which he found himself, my old acquaintance did not so much excite sympathy in me as it did a sort of unfavorable sentiment.

I now vividly remembered our first meeting. In 1848, while I was staying at Moscow, I frequently went to the house of Ivashin, who from childhood had been an old friend of mine. His wife was an agreeable hostess, a charming woman, as everybody said; but she never pleased me. . . . The winter that I knew her, she often spoke with hardly concealed pride of her brother, who had shortly before completed his course, and promised to be one of the most fashionable and popular young men in the best society of Petersburg. As I knew by reputation the father of the Guskofs, who was very rich and had a distinguished position, and as I knew also the sister's ways, I felt some prejudice against meeting the young man. One evening when I was at Ivashin's, I saw a short, thoroughly pleasant-looking young man, in a black coat, white vest and necktie. My host hastened to make me acquainted with him. The young man, evidently dressed for a ball, with his cap in his hand, was standing before Ivashin, and was eagerly but politely arguing with him about a common friend of ours, who had distinguished himself at the time of the Hungarian campaign. He said that this acquaintance was not at all a hero or a man born for war, as was said of him, but was simply a clever and cultivated man. I recollect, I took part in the argument against Guskof, and went to the extreme of declaring also that intellect and cultivation always bore an inverse relation to bravery; and I recollect how Guskof pleasantly and cleverly pointed out to me that bravery was necessarily the result of intellect and a decided degree of development,--a statement which I, who considered myself an intellectual and cultivated man, could not in my heart of hearts agree with.

I recollect that towards the close of our conversation Madame Ivashina introduced me to her brother; and he, with a condescending smile, offered me his little hand on which he had not yet had time to draw his kid gloves, and weakly and irresolutely pressed my hand as he did now. Though I had been prejudiced against Guskof, I could not help granting that he was in the right, and agreeing with his sister that he was really a clever and agreeable young man, who ought to have great success in society. He was extraordinarily neat, beautifully dressed, and fresh, and had affectedly modest manners, and a thoroughly youthful, almost childish appearance, on account of which you could not help excusing his expression of self-sufficiency, though it modified the impression of his high-mightiness caused by his intellectual face and especially his smile. It is said that he had great success that winter with the high- born ladies of Moscow. As I saw him at his sister's I could only infer how far this was true by the feeling of pleasure and contentment constantly excited in me by his youthful appearance and by his sometimes indiscreet anecdotes. He and I met half a dozen times, and talked a good deal; or, rather, he talked a good deal, and I listened. He spoke for the most part in French, always with a good accent, very fluently and ornately; and he had the skill of drawing others gently and politely into the conversation. As a general thing, he behaved toward all, and toward me, in a somewhat supercilious manner, and I felt that he was perfectly right in this way of treating people. I always feel that way in regard to men who are firmly convinced that they ought to treat me superciliously, and who are comparative strangers to me.

Now, as he sat with me, and gave me his hand, I keenly recalled in him that same old haughtiness of expression; and it seemed to me that he did not properly appreciate his position of official inferiority, as, in the presence of the officers, he asked me what I had been doing in all that time, and how I happened to be there. In spite of the fact that I invariably made my replies in Russian, he kept putting his questions in French, expressing himself as before in remarkably correct language. About himself he said fluently that after his unhappy, wretched story (what the story was, I did not know, and he had not yet told me), he had been three months under arrest, and then had been sent to the Caucasus to the N. regiment, and now had been serving three years as a soldier in that regiment.

"You would not believe," said he to me in French, "how much I have to suffer in these regiments from the society of the officers. Still it is a pleasure to me, that I used to know the adjutant of whom we were just speaking: he is a good man--it's a fact," he remarked condescendingly. "I live with him, and that's something of a relief for me. Yes, my dear, the days fly by, but they aren't all alike,"[20] he added; and suddenly hesitated, reddened, and stood up, as he caught sight of the adjutant himself coming toward us.

"It is such a pleasure to meet such a man as you," said Guskof to me in a whisper as he turned from me. "I should like very, very much, to have a long talk with you."

I said that I should be very happy to talk with him, but in reality I confess that Guskof excited in me a sort of dull pity that was not akin to sympathy.

I had a presentiment that I should feel a constraint in a private conversation with him; but still I was anxious to learn from him several things, and, above all, why it was, when his father had been so rich, that he was in poverty, as was evident by his dress and appearance.

The adjutant greeted us all, including Guskof, and sat down by me in the seat which the cashiered officer had just vacated. Pavel Dmitrievitch, who had always been calm and leisurely, a genuine gambler, and a man of means, was now very different from what he had been in the flowery days of his success; he seemed to

20   OUI, MON CHER, LES JOURS SE SUIVENT, MAIS NE SE RESSEMBLENT PAS: in French in the original.

be in haste to go somewhere, kept constantly glancing at everybody, and it was not five minutes before he proposed to Lieutenant O., who had sworn off from playing, to set up a small faro-bank. Lieutenant O. refused, under the pretext of having to attend to his duties, but in reality because, as he knew that the adjutant had few possessions and little money left, he did not feel himself justified in risking his three hundred rubles against a hundred or even less which the adjutant might stake.

"Well, Pavel Dmitrievitch," said the lieutenant, anxious to avoid a repetition of the invitation, "is it true, what they tell us, that we return to-morrow?"

"I don't know," replied the adjutant. "Orders came to be in readiness; but if it's true, then you'd better play a game. I would wager my Kabarda cloak."

"No, to-day already" . . .

"It's a gray one, never been worn; but if you prefer, play for money. How is that?"

"Yes, but . . . I should be willing--pray don't think that" . . . said Lieutenant O., answering the implied suspicion; "but as there may be a raid or some movement, I must go to bed early."

The adjutant stood up, and, thrusting his hands into his pockets, started to go across the grounds. His face assumed its ordinary expression of coldness and pride, which I admired in him.

"Won't you have a glass of mulled wine?" I asked him.

"That might be acceptable," and he came back to me; but Guskof politely took the glass from me, and handed it to the adjutant, striving at the same time not to look at him. But as he did not notice the tent-rope, he stumbled over it, and fell on his hand, dropping the glass.

"What a bungler!" exclaimed the adjutant, still holding out his hand for the glass. Everybody burst out laughing, not excepting Guskof, who was rubbing his hand on his sore knee, which he had somehow struck as he fell. "That's the way the bear waited on the hermit," continued the adjutant. "It's the way he waits on me every day. He has pulled up all the tent-pins; he's always tripping up."

Guskof, not hearing him, apologized to us, and glanced toward me with a smile of almost noticeable melancholy, as though saying that I alone could understand him. He was pitiable to see; but the adjutant, his protector, seemed, on that very account, to be severe on his messmate, and did not try to put him at his ease.

"Well, you're a graceful lad! Where did you think you were going?"

"Well, who can help tripping over these pins, Pavel Dmitrievitch?" said Guskof. "You tripped over them yourself the other day."

"I, old man,[21]--I am not of the rank and file, and such gracefulness is not expected of me."

"He can be lazy," said Captain S., keeping the ball rolling, "but low- rank men have to make their legs fly."

"Ill-timed jest," said Guskof, almost in a whisper, and casting down his eyes. The adjutant was evidently vexed with his messmate; he listened with inquisitive attention to every word that he said.

"He'll have to be sent out into ambuscade again," said he, addressing S., and pointing to the cashiered officer.

"Well, there'll be some more tears," said S., laughing. Guskof no longer looked at me, but acted as though he were going to take some tobacco from his pouch, though there had been none there for some time.

"Get ready for the ambuscade, old man," said S., addressing him with shouts of laughter. "To-day the scouts have brought the news, there'll be an attack on the camp to-night, so it's necessary to designate the trusty lads." Guskof's face showed a fleeting smile as though he were preparing to make some reply, but several times he cast a supplicating look at S.

"Well, you know I have been, and I'm ready to go again if I am sent," he said hastily.

"Then you'll be sent."

"Well, I'll go. Isn't that all right?"

"Yes, as at Arguna, you deserted the ambuscade and threw away your gun," said the adjutant; and turning from him he began to tell us the orders for the next day.

As a matter of fact, we expected from the enemy a cannonade of the camp that night, and the next day some sort of diversion. While we were still chatting about various subjects of general interest, the adjutant, as though from a sudden and unexpected impulse, proposed to Lieutenant O. to have a little game. The lieutenant most unexpectedly consented; and, together with S. and the ensign, they went off

---

21 batiushka

to the adjutant's tent, where there was a folding green table with cards on it. The captain, the commander of our division, went to our tent to sleep; the other gentlemen also separated, and Guskof and I were left alone. I was not mistaken, it was really very uncomfortable for me to have a tete-a-tete with him; I arose involuntarily, and began to promenade up and down on the battery. Guskof walked in silence by my side, hastily and awkwardly wheeling around so as not to delay or incommode me.

"I do not annoy you?" he asked in a soft, mournful voice. So far as I could see his face in the dim light, it seemed to me deeply thoughtful and melancholy.

"Not at all," I replied; but as he did not immediately begin to speak, and as I did not know what to say to him, we walked in silence a considerably long time.

The twilight had now absolutely changed into dark night; over the black profile of the mountains gleamed the bright evening heat-lightning; over our heads in the light-blue frosty sky twinkled the little stars; on all sides gleamed the ruddy flames of the smoking watch-fires; near us, the white tents stood out in contrast to the frowning blackness of our earth-works. The light from the nearest watch-fire, around which our servants, engaged in quiet conversation, were warming themselves, occasionally flashed on the brass of our heavy guns, and fell on the form of the sentry, who, wrapped in his cloak, paced with measured tread along the battery.

"You cannot imagine what a delight it is for me to talk with such a man as you are," said Guskof, although as yet he had not spoken a word to me. "Only one who had been in my position could appreciate it."

I did not know how to reply to him, and we again relapsed into silence, although it was evident that he was anxious to talk and have me listen to him.

"Why were you . . . why did you suffer this?" I inquired at last, not being able to invent any better way of breaking the ice.

"Why, didn't you hear about this wretched business from Metenin?"

"Yes, a duel, I believe; I did not hear much about it," I replied. "You see, I have been for some time in the Caucasus."

"No, it wasn't a duel, but it was a stupid and horrid story. I will tell you all about it, if you don't know. It happened that the same year that I met you at my sister's I was living at Petersburg. I must tell you I had then what they call une position dans le monde,--a position good enough if it was not brilliant. Mon pere me donnait ten thousand par an. In '49 I was promised a place in the embassy at Turin; my uncle on my mother's side had influence, and was always ready to do a great deal for me. That sort of thing is all past now. J'etais recu dans la meilleure societe de Petersburg; I might have aspired to any girl in the city. I was well educated, as we all are who come from the school, but was not especially cultivated; to be sure, I read a good deal afterwards, mais j'avais surtout, you know, ce jargon du monde, and, however it came about, I was looked upon as a leading light among the young men of Petersburg. What raised me more than all in common estimation, c'est cette liaison avec Madame D., about which a great deal was said in Petersburg; but I was frightfully young at that time, and did not prize these advantages very highly. I was simply young and stupid. What more did I need? Just then that Metenin had some notoriety--"

And Guskof went on in the same fashion to relate to me the history of his misfortunes, which I will omit, as it would not be at all interesting.

"Two months I remained under arrest," he continued, "absolutely alone; and what thoughts did I not have during that time? But, you know, when it was all over, as though every tie had been broken with the past, then it became easier for me. Mon pere,--you have heard tell of him, of course, a man of iron will and strong convictions,--il m'a desherite, and broken off all intercourse with me. According to his convictions he had to do as he did, and I don't blame him at all. He was consistent. Consequently, I have not taken a step to induce him to change his mind. My sister was abroad. Madame D. is the only one who wrote to me when I was released, and she sent me assistance; but you understand that I could not accept it, so that I had none of those little things which make one's position a little easier, you know,--books, linen, food, nothing at all. At this time I thought things over and over, and began to look at life with different eyes. For instance, this noise, this society gossip about me in Petersburg, did not interest me, did not flatter me; it all seemed to me ridiculous. I felt that I myself had been to blame; I was young and indiscreet; I had spoiled my career, and I only thought how I might get into the right track again. And I felt that I had strength and energy enough for it. After my arrest, as I told you, I was sent here to the Caucasus to the N. regiment.

"I thought," he went on to say, all the time becoming more and more animated,--"I thought that here in the Caucasus, la vie de camp, the simple, honest men with whom I should associate, and war and danger, would all admirably agree with my mental state, so that I might begin a new life. They will see me under fire.[22] I shall make myself liked; I shall be respected for my real self,--the cross--non-commissioned officer; they will relieve me of my fine; and I shall get up again, et vous savez avec ce prestige du malheur! But, quel desenchantement! You can't imagine how I have been deceived! You know what sort of men the officers of our regiment are."

He did not speak for some little time, waiting, as it appeared, for me to tell him that I knew the society of our officers here was bad; but I made him no reply. It went against my grain that he should expect me, because I knew French, forsooth, to be obliged to take issue with the society of the officers, which, during my long residence in the Caucasus, I had had time enough to appreciate fully, and for which I had far higher respect than for the society from which Mr. Guskof had sprung. I wanted to tell him so, but his position constrained me.

"In the N. regiment the society of the officers is a thousand times worse than it is here," he continued. "I hope that it is saying a good deal; J'ESPERE QUE C'EST BEAUCOUP DIRE; that is, you cannot imagine what it is. I am not speaking of the yunkers and the soldiers. That is horrible, it is so bad. At first they received me very kindly, that is absolutely the truth; but when they saw that I could not help despising them, you know, in these inconceivably small circumstances, they saw that I was a man absolutely different, standing far above them, they got angry with me, and began to put various little humiliations on me. You haven't an idea what I had to suffer.[23] Then this forced relationship with the yunkers, and especially with the small means that I had--I lacked everything;[24] I had only what my sister used to send me. And here's a proof for you! As much as it made me suffer, I with my character, AVEC MA FIERTE J'AI ECRIS A MON PERE, begged him to send me something. I understand how living four years of such a life may make a man like our cashiered Dromof who drinks with soldiers, and writes notes to all the officers asking them to loan him three rubles, and signing it, TOUT A VOUS, DROMOF. One must have such a character as I have, not to be mired in the least by such a horrible position."

For some time he walked in silence by my side.

22   On me verra au feu.
23   CE QUE J'AI EUA SOUFFRIR VOUS NE FAITES PAS UNE IDEE.
24   AVEC LES PETITS MOYENS QUE J'AVAIS, JE MANQUAIS DE TOUT

"Have you a cigarette?"[25] he asked me.

"And so I stayed right where I was? Yes. I could not endure it physically, because, though we were wretched, cold, and ill-fed, I lived like a common soldier, but still the officers had some sort of consideration for me. I had still some prestige that they regarded. I wasn't sent out on guard nor for drill. I could not have stood that. But morally my sufferings were frightful; and especially because I didn't see any escape from my position. I wrote my uncle, begged him to get me transferred to my present regiment, which, at least, sees some service; and I thought that here Pavel Dmitrievitch, qui est le fils de l'intendant de mon pere, might be of some use to me. My uncle did this for me; I was transferred. After that regiment this one seemed to me a collection of chamberlains. Then Pavel Dmitrievitch was here; he knew who I was, and I was splendidly received. At my uncle's request--a Guskof, vous savez; but I forgot that with these men without cultivation and undeveloped,--they can't appreciate a man, and show him marks of esteem, unless he has that aureole of wealth, of friends; and I noticed how, little by little, when they saw that I was poor, their behavior to me showed more and more indifference until they have come almost to despise me. It is horrible, but it is absolutely the truth.

"Here I have been in action, I have fought, they have seen me under fire,"[26] he continued; "but when will it all end? I think, never. And my strength and energy have already begun to flag. Then I had imagined la guerre, la vie de camp; but it isn't at all what I see, in a sheepskin jacket, dirty linen, soldier's boots, and you go out in ambuscade, and the whole night long lie in the ditch with some Antonof reduced to the ranks for drunkenness, and any minute from behind the bush may come a rifle-shot and hit you or Antonof,--it's all the same which. That is not bravery; it's horrible, c'est affreux, it's killing!"[27]

"Well, you can be promoted a non-commissioned officer for this campaign, and next year an ensign," said I.

"Yes, it may be: they promised me that in two years, and it's not up yet. What would those two years amount to, if I knew any one! You can imagine this life with Pavel Dmitrievitch; cards, low jokes, drinking all the time; if you wish to tell anything that is weighing on your mind, you would not be understood, or you would

25   "Avez-vous un papiros?"

26   On m'a vu au feu.

27   Ca tue

be laughed at: they talk with you, not for the sake of sharing a thought, but to get something funny out of you. Yes, and so it has gone--in a brutal, beastly way, and you are always conscious that you belong to the rank and file; they always make you feel that. Hence you can't realize what an enjoyment it is to talk a coeur ouvert to such a man as you are."

I had never imagined what kind of a man I was, and consequently I did not know what answer to make him.

"Will you have your lunch now?" asked Nikita at this juncture, approaching me unseen in the darkness, and, as I could perceive, vexed at the presence of a guest. "Nothing but curd dumplings, there's none of the roast beef left."

"Has the captain had his lunch yet?"

"He went to bed long ago," replied Nikita, gruffly, "According to my directions, I was to bring you lunch here and your brandy." He muttered something else discontentedly, and sauntered off to his tent. After loitering a while longer, he brought us, nevertheless, a lunch-case; he placed a candle on the lunch-case, and shielded it from the wind with a sheet of paper. He brought a saucepan, some mustard in a jar, a tin dipper with a handle, and a bottle of absinthe. After arranging these things, Nikita lingered around us for some moments, and looked on as Guskof and I were drinking the liquor, and it was evidently very distasteful to him. By the feeble light shed by the candle through the paper, amid the encircling darkness, could be seen the seal-skin cover of the lunch-case, the supper arranged upon it, Guskof's sheepskin jacket, his face, and his small red hands which he used in lifting the patties from the pan. Everything around us was black; and only by straining the sight could be seen the dark battery, the dark form of the sentry moving along the breastwork, on all sides the watch-fires, and on high the ruddy stars.

Guskof wore a melancholy, almost guilty smile as though it were awkward for him to look into my face after his confession. He drank still another glass of liquor, and ate ravenously, emptying the saucepan.

"Yes; for you it must be a relief all the same," said I, for the sake of saying something,--"your acquaintance with the adjutant. He is a very good man, I have heard."

"Yes," replied the cashiered officer, "he is a kind man; but he can't help being what he is, with his education, and it is useless to expect it."

A flush seemed suddenly to cross his face. "You remarked his coarse jest this evening about the ambuscade;" and Guskof, though I tried several times to interrupt him, began to justify himself before me, and to show that he had not run away from the ambuscade, and that he was not a coward as the adjutant and Capt. S. tried to make him out.

"As I was telling you," he went on to say, wiping his hands on his jacket, "such people can't show any delicacy toward a man, a common soldier, who hasn't much money either. That's beyond their strength. And here recently, while I haven't received anything at all from my sister, I have been conscious that they have changed toward me. This sheepskin jacket, which I bought of a soldier, and which hasn't any warmth in it, because it's all worn off" (and here he showed me where the wool was gone from the inside), "it doesn't arouse in him any sympathy or consideration for my unhappiness, but scorn, which he does not take pains to hide. Whatever my necessities may be, as now when I have nothing to eat except soldiers' gruel, and nothing to wear," he continued, casting down his eyes, and pouring out for himself still another glass of liquor, "he does not even offer to lend me some money, though he knows perfectly well that I would give it back to him; but he waits till I am obliged to ask him for it. But you appreciate how it is for me to go to him. In your case I should say, square and fair, vous etes audessus de cela, mon cher, je n'ai pas le sou. And you know," said he, looking straight into my eyes with an expression of desperation, "I am going to tell you, square and fair, I am in a terrible situation: pouvez-vous me preter dix rubles argent? My sister ought to send me some by the mail, et mon pere--"

"Why, most willingly," said I, although, on the contrary, it was trying and unpleasant, especially because the evening before, having lost at cards, I had left only about five rubles in Nikita's care. "In a moment," said I, arising, "I will go and get it at the tent."

"No, by and by: ne vous derangez pas."

Nevertheless, not heeding him, I hastened to the closed tent, where stood my bed, and where the captain was sleeping.

"Aleksei Ivanuitch, let me have ten rubles, please, for rations," said I to the captain, shaking him.

"What! have you been losing again? But this very evening, you were not going to play any more," murmured the captain, still half asleep.

"No, I have not been playing; but I want the money; let me have it, please."

"Makatiuk!" shouted the captain to his servant,[28] "hand me my bag with the money."

"Hush, hush!" said I, hearing Guskof's measured steps near the tent.

"What? Why hush?"

"Because that cashiered fellow has asked to borrow it of me. He's right there."

"Well, if you knew him, you wouldn't let him have it," remarked the captain. "I have heard about him. He's a dirty, low-lived fellow."

Nevertheless, the captain gave me the money, ordered his man to put away the bag, pulled the flap of the tent neatly to, and, again saying, "If you only knew him, you wouldn't let him have it," drew his head down under the coverlet. "Now you owe me thirty-two, remember," he shouted after me.

When I came out of the tent, Guskof was walking near the settees; and his slight figure, with his crooked legs, his shapeless cap, his long white hair, kept appearing and disappearing in the darkness, as he passed in and out of the light of the candles. He made believe not to see me.

I handed him the money. He said "Merci," and, crumpling the bank-bill, thrust it into his trousers pocket.

"Now I suppose the game is in full swing at the adjutant's," he began immediately after this.

"Yes, I suppose so."

"He's a wonderful player, always bold, and never backs out. When he's in luck, it's fine; but when it does not go well with him, he can lose frightfully. He has given proof of that. During this expedition, if you reckon his valuables, he has lost more than fifteen hundred rubles. But, as he played discreetly before, that officer of yours seemed to have some doubts about his honor."

"Well, that's because he . . . Nikita, haven't we any of that red Kavkas wine[29] left?" I asked, very much enlivened by Guskof's conversational talent. Nikita still kept muttering; but he brought us the red wine, and again looked on angrily as Guskof drained his glass. In Guskof's behavior was noticeable his old freedom from constraint. I wished that he would go as soon as possible; it seemed as if his only

28   Denshchik
29   Chikir

reason for not going was because he did not wish to go immediately after receiving the money. I said nothing.

"How could you, who have means, and were under no necessity, simply de gaiete de coeur, make up your mind to come and serve in the Caucasus? That's what I don't understand," said he to me.

I endeavored to explain this act of renunciation, which seemed so strange to him.

"I can imagine how disagreeable the society of those officers--men without any comprehension of culture--must be for you. You could not understand each other. You see, you might live ten years, and not see anything, and not hear about anything, except cards, wine, and gossip about rewards and campaigns."

It was unpleasant for me, that he wished me to put myself on a par with him in his position; and, with absolute honesty, I assured him that I was very fond of cards and wine, and gossip about campaigns, and that I did not care to have any better comrades than those with whom I was associated. But he would not believe me.

"Well, you may say so," he continued; "but the lack of women's society,-- I mean, of course, FEMMES COMME IL FAUT,--is that not a terrible deprivation? I don't know what I would give now to go into a parlor, if only for a moment, and to have a look at a pretty woman, even though it were through a crack."

He said nothing for a little, and drank still another glass of the red wine.

"Oh, my God, my God![30] If it only might be our fate to meet again, somewhere in Petersburg, to live and move among men, among ladies!"

He drank up the dregs of the wine still left in the bottle, and when he had finished it he said: "AKH! PARDON, maybe you wanted some more. It was horribly careless of me. However, I suppose I must have taken too much, and my head isn't very strong.[31] There was a time when I lived on Morskaia Street, AU REZ-DE-CHAUSSEE, and had marvellous apartments, furniture, you know, and I was able to arrange it all beautifully, not so very expensively though; my father, to be sure, gave me porcelains, flowers, and silver--a wonderful lot. Le matin je sortais, visits, 5 heures regulierement. I used to go and dine with her; often she was alone. Il faut avouer que c'etait une femme ravissante! You didn't know her at all, did you?"

"No."

---

30 AKH, BOZHE MOI, BOZHE MOI.
31 ET JE N'AI PAS LA TETE FORTE.

"You see, there was such high degree of womanliness in her, and such tenderness, and what love! Lord! I did not know how to appreciate my happiness then. We would return after the theatre, and have a little supper together. It was never dull where she was, toujours gaie, toujours aimante. Yes, and I had never imagined what rare happiness it was. Et j'ai beaucoup a me reprocher in regard to her. Je l'ai fait souffrir et souvent. I was outrageous. AKH! What a marvellous time that was! Do I bore you?"

"No, not at all."

"Then I will tell you about our evenings. I used to go--that stairway, every flower-pot I knew,--the door-handle, all was so lovely, so familiar; then the vestibule, her room. . . . No, it will never, never come back to me again! Even now she writes to me: if you will let me, I will show you her letters. But I am not what I was; I am ruined; I am no longer worthy of her. . . . Yes, I am ruined for ever. Je suis casse. There's no energy in me, no pride, nothing--nor even any rank. . . .[32] Yes, I am ruined; and no one will ever appreciate my sufferings. Every one is indifferent. I am a lost man. Never any chance for me to rise, because I have fallen morally . . . into the mire--I have fallen. . . ."

At this moment there was evident in his words a genuine, deep despair: he did not look at me, but sat motionless.

"Why are you in such despair?" I asked.

"Because I am abominable. This life has degraded me, all that was in me, all is crushed out. It is not by pride that I hold out, but by abjectness: there's no dignite dans le malheur. I am humiliated every moment; I endure it all; I got myself into this abasement. This mire has soiled me. I myself have become coarse; I have forgotten what I used to know; I can't speak French any more; I am conscious that I am base and low. I cannot tear myself away from these surroundings, indeed I cannot. I might have been a hero: give me a regiment, gold epaulets, a trumpeter, but to march in the ranks with some wild Anton Bondarenko or the like, and feel that between me and him there was no difference at all--that he might be killed or I might be killed--all the same, that thought is maddening. You understand how horrible it is to think that some ragamuffin may kill me, a man who has thoughts and feelings, and that it would make no difference if alongside of me some Antonof

---

32 Blagorodstva, noble birth, nobility.

were killed,--a being not different from an animal--and that it might easily happen that I and not this Antonof were killed, which is always UNE FATALITE for every lofty and good man. I know that they call me a coward: grant that I am a coward, I certainly am a coward, and can't be anything else. Not only am I a coward, but I am in my way a low and despicable man. Here I have just been borrowing money of you, and you have the right to despise me. No, take back your money." And he held out to me the crumpled bank-bill. "I want you to have a good opinion of me." He covered his face with his hands, and burst into tears. I really did not know what to say or do.

"Calm yourself," I said to him. "You are too sensitive; don't take everything so to heart; don't indulge in self-analysis, look at things more simply. You yourself say that you have character. Keep up good heart, you won't have long to wait," I said to him, but not very consistently, because I was much stirred both by a feeling of sympathy and a feeling of repentance, because I had allowed myself mentally to sin in my judgment of a man truly and deeply unhappy.

"Yes," he began, "if I had heard even once, at the time when I was in that hell, one single word of sympathy, of advice, of friendship--one humane word such as you have just spoken, perhaps I might have calmly endured all; perhaps I might have struggled, and been a soldier. But now this is horrible. . . . When I think soberly, I long for death. Why should I love my despicable life and my own self, now that I am ruined for all that is worth while in the world? And at the least danger, I suddenly, in spite of myself, begin to pray for my miserable life, and to watch over it as though it were precious, and I cannot, je ne puis pas, control myself. That is, I could," he continued again after a minute's silence, "but this is too hard work for me, a monstrous work, when I am alone. With others, under special circumstances, when you are going into action, I am brave, j'ai fait mes epreuves, because I am vain and proud: that is my failing, and in presence of others. . . . Do you know, let me spend the night with you: with us, they will play all night long; it makes no difference, anywhere, on the ground."

While Nikita was making the bed, we got up, and once more began to walk up and down in the darkness on the battery. Certainly Guskof's head must have been very weak, because two glasses of liquor and two of wine made him dizzy. As we got up and moved away from the candles, I noticed that he again thrust the ten-ruble bill into his pocket, trying to do so without my seeing it. During all the foregoing conversation, he had held it in his hand. He continued to reiterate how he felt that he might regain his old station if he had a man such as I were to take some interest in him.

We were just going into the tent to go to bed when suddenly a cannon- ball whistled over us, and buried itself in the ground not far from us. So strange it was,--that peacefully sleeping camp, our conversation, and suddenly the hostile cannon-ball which flew from God knows where, the midst of our tents,--so strange that it was some time before I could realize what it was. Our sentinel, Andreief, walking up and down on the battery, moved toward me.

"Ha! he's crept up to us. It was the fire here that he aimed at," said he.

"We must rouse the captain," said I, and gazed at Guskof.

He stood cowering close to the ground, and stammered, trying to say, "Th-that's th-the ene-my's . . . f-f-fire--th-that's--hidi--." Further he could not say a word, and I did not see how and where he disappeared so instantaneously.

In the captain's tent a candle gleamed; his cough, which always troubled him when he was awake, was heard; and he himself soon appeared, asking for a linstock to light his little pipe.

"What does this mean, old man?"[33] he asked with a smile. "Aren't they willing to give me a little sleep to-night? First it's you with your cashiered friend, and then it's Shamyl. What shall we do, answer him or not? There was nothing about this in the instructions, was there?"

"Nothing at all. There he goes again," said I. "Two of them!"

Indeed, in the darkness, directly in front of us, flashed two fires, like two eyes; and quickly over our heads flew one cannon-ball and one heavy shell. It must have been meant for us, coming with a loud and penetrating hum. From the neighboring tents the soldiers hastened. You could hear them hawking and talking and stretching themselves.

"Hist! the fuse sings like a nightingale," was the remark of the artillerist.

"Send for Nikita," said the captain with his perpetually benevolent smile. "Nikita, don't hide yourself, but listen to the mountain nightingales."

"Well, your honor,"[34] said Nikita, who was standing near the captain, "I have

33 Batiushka
34 VASHE VUISOKOBLAGORODIE. German, HOCHWOHLGEBORENER, high, well-born;

seen them--these nightingales. I am not afraid of 'em; but here was that stranger who was here, he was drinking up your red wine. When he heard how that shot dashed by our tents, and the shell rolled by, he cowered down like some wild beast."

"However, we must send to the commander of the artillery," said the captain to me, in a serious tone of authority, "and ask whether we shall reply to the fire or not. It will probably be nothing at all, but still it may. Have the goodness to go and ask him. Have a horse saddled. Do it as quickly as possible, even if you take my Polkan."

In five minutes they brought me a horse, and I galloped off to the commander of the artillery. "Look you, return on foot," whispered the punctilious captain, "else they won't let you through the lines."

It was half a verst to the artillery commander's, the whole road ran between the tents. As soon as I rode away from our fire, it became so black that I could not see even the horse's ears, but only the watch- fires, now seeming very near, now very far off, as they gleamed into my eyes. After I had ridden some distance, trusting to the intelligence of the horse whom I allowed free rein, I began to distinguish the white four-cornered tents and then the black tracks of the road. After a half-hour, having asked my way three times, and twice stumbled over the tent- stakes, causing each time a volley of curses from the tents, and twice been detained by the sentinels, I reached the artillery commander's. While I was on the way, I heard two more cannon shot in the direction of our camp; but the projectiles did not reach to the place where the headquarters were. The artillery commander ordered not to reply to the firing, the more as the enemy did not remain in the same place; and I went back, leading the horse by the bridle, making my way on foot between the infantry tents. More than once I delayed my steps, as I went by some soldier's tent where a light was shining, and some merry-andrew was telling a story; or I listened to some educated soldier reading from some book while the whole division overflowed the tent, or hung around it, sometimes interrupting the reading with various remarks; or I simply listened to the talk about the expedition, about the fatherland, or about their chiefs.

As I came around one of the tents of the third battalion, I heard Guskof's rough voice: he was speaking hilariously and rapidly. Young voices replied to him, not

---

regulation title of officers from major to general

those of soldiers, but of gay gentlemen. It was evidently the tent of some yunker or sergeant-major. I stopped short.

"I've known him a long time," Guskof was saying. "When I lived in Petersburg, he used to come to my house often; and I went to his. He moved in the best society."

"Whom are you talking about?" asked the drunken voice.

"About the prince," said Guskof. "We were relatives, you see, but, more than all, we were old friends. It's a mighty good thing, you know, gentlemen, to have such an acquaintance. You see he's fearfully rich. To him a hundred silver rubles is a mere bagatelle. Here, I just got a little money out of him, enough to last me till my sister sends."

"Let's have some."

"Right away.--Savelitch, my dear," said Guskof, coming to the door of the tent, "here's ten rubles for you: go to the sutler, get two bottles of Kakhetinski. Anything else, gentlemen? What do you say?" and Guskof, with unsteady gait, with dishevelled hair, without his hat, came out of the tent. Throwing open his jacket, and thrusting his hands into the pockets of his trousers, he stood at the door of the tent. Though he was in the light, and I in darkness; I trembled with fear lest he should see me, and I went on, trying to make no noise.

"Who goes there?" shouted Guskof after me in a thoroughly drunken voice. Apparently, the cold took hold of him. "Who the devil is going off with that horse?"

I made no answer, and silently went on my way.

The Codes Of Hammurabi And Moses
W. W. Davies

QTY

The discovery of the Hammurabi Code is one of the greatest achievements of archaeology, and is of paramount interest, not only to the student of the Bible, but also to all those interested in ancient history...

Religion   ISBN: *1-59462-338-4*   Pages:132
MSRP $12.95

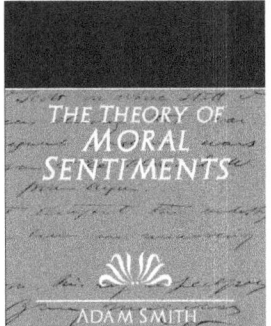

The Theory of Moral Sentiments
Adam Smith

QTY

This work from 1749. contains original theories of conscience amd moral judgment and it is the foundation for systemof morals.

Philosophy ISBN: *1-59462-777-0*   Pages:536
MSRP $19.95

Jessica's First Prayer
Hesba Stretton

QTY

In a screened and secluded corner of one of the many railway-bridges which span the streets of London there could be seen a few years ago, from five o'clock every morning until half past eight, a tidily set-out coffee-stall, consisting of a trestle and board, upon which stood two large tin cans, with a small fire of charcoal burning under each so as to keep the coffee boiling during the early hours of the morning when the work-people were thronging into the city on their way to their daily toil...

Childrens   ISBN: *1-59462-373-2*   Pages:84
MSRP $9.95

My Life and Work
Henry Ford

QTY

Henry Ford revolutionized the world with his implementation of mass production for the Model T automobile. Gain valuable business insight into his life and work with his own auto-biography... "We have only started on our development of our country we have not as yet, with all our talk of wonderful progress, done more than scratch the surface. The progress has been wonderful enough but..."

Biographies/   ISBN: *1-59462-198-5*   Pages:300
MSRP $21.95

The Art of Cross-Examination
Francis Wellman

QTY

I presume it is the experience of every author, after his first book is published upon an important subject, to be almost overwhelmed with a wealth of ideas and illustrations which could readily have been included in his book, and which to his own mind, at least, seem to make a second edition inevitable. Such certainly was the case with me; and when the first edition had reached its sixth impression in five months, I rejoiced to learn that it seemed to my publishers that the book had met with a sufficiently favorable reception to justify a second and considerably enlarged edition. ..

Pages:412

Reference   ISBN: *1-59462-647-2*   *MSRP $19.95*

On the Duty of Civil Disobedience
Henry David Thoreau

QTY

Thoreau wrote his famous essay, On the Duty of Civil Disobedience, as a protest against an unjust but popular war and the immoral but popular institution of slave-owning. He did more than write—he declined to pay his taxes, and was hauled off to gaol in consequence. Who can say how much this refusal of his hastened the end of the war and of slavery ?

Law   ISBN: *1-59462-747-9*   **Pages:48**

MSRP $7.45

Dream Psychology Psychoanalysis for Beginners
Sigmund Freud

QTY

Sigmund Freud, born Sigismund Schlomo Freud (May 6, 1856 - September 23, 1939), was a Jewish-Austrian neurologist and psychiatrist who co-founded the psychoanalytic school of psychology. Freud is best known for his theories of the unconscious mind, especially involving the mechanism of repression; his redefinition of sexual desire as mobile and directed towards a wide variety of objects; and his therapeutic techniques, especially his understanding of transference in the therapeutic relationship and the presumed value of dreams as sources of insight into unconscious desires.

Pages:196

Psychology   ISBN: *1-59462-905-6*   *MSRP $15.45*

The Miracle of Right Thought
Orison Swett Marden

QTY

Believe with all of your heart that you will do what you were made to do. When the mind has once formed the habit of holding cheerful, happy, prosperous pictures, it will not be easy to form the opposite habit. It does not matter how improbable or how far away this realization may see, or how dark the prospects may be, if we visualize them as best we can, as vividly as possible, hold tenaciously to them and vigorously struggle to attain them, they will gradually become actualized, realized in the life. But a desire, a longing without endeavor, a yearning abandoned or held indifferently will vanish without realization.

Pages:360

Self Help   ISBN: *1-59462-644-8*   *MSRP $25.45*

QTY

The Rosicrucian Cosmo-Conception Mystic Christianity *by Max Heindel*   ISBN: *1-59462-188-8*   **$38.95**
The Rosicrucian Cosmo-conception is not dogmatic, neither does it appeal to any other authority than the reason of the student. It is: not controversial, but is: sent forth in the, hope that it may help to clear...   New Age/Religion Pages 646

Abandonment To Divine Providence *by Jean-Pierre de Caussade*   ISBN: *1-59462-228-0*   **$25.95**
"The Rev. Jean Pierre de Caussade was one of the most remarkable spiritual writers of the Society of Jesus in France in the 18th Century. His death took place at Toulouse in 1751. His works have gone through many editions and have been republished...   Inspirational/Religion Pages 400

Mental Chemistry *by Charles Haanel*   ISBN: *1-59462-192-6*   **$23.95**
Mental Chemistry allows the change of material conditions by combining and appropriately utilizing the power of the mind. Much like applied chemistry creates something new and unique out of careful combinations of chemicals the mastery of mental chemistry...   New Age Pages 354

The Letters of Robert Browning and Elizabeth Barret Barrett 1845-1846 vol II   ISBN: *1-59462-193-4*   **$35.95**
by Robert Browning and Elizabeth Barrett   Biographies Pages 596

Gleanings In Genesis (volume I) *by Arthur W. Pink*   ISBN: *1-59462-130-6*   **$27.45**
Appropriately has Genesis been termed "the seed plot of the Bible" for in it we have, in germ form, almost all of the great doctrines which are afterwards fully developed in the books of Scripture which follow...   Religion/Inspirational Pages 420

The Master Key *by L. W. de Laurence*   ISBN: *1-59462-001-6*   **$30.95**
In no branch of human knowledge has there been a more lively increase of the spirit of research during the past few years than in the study of Psychology, Concentration and Mental Discipline. The requests for authentic lessons in Thought Control, Mental Discipline and...   New Age/Business Pages 422

The Lesser Key Of Solomon Goetia *by L. W. de Laurence*   ISBN: *1-59462-092-X*   **$9.95**
This translation of the first book of the "Lemegton" which is now for the first time made accessible to students of Talismanic Magic was done, after careful collation and edition, from numerous Ancient Manuscripts in Hebrew, Latin, and French...   New Age/Occult Pages 92

Rubaiyat Of Omar Khayyam *by Edward Fitzgerald*   ISBN:*1-59462-332-5*   **$13.95**
Edward Fitzgerald, whom the world has already learned, in spite of his own efforts to remain within the shadow of anonymity, to look upon as one of the rarest poets of the century, was born at Bredfield, in Suffolk, on the 31st of March, 1809. He was the third son of John Purcell...   Music Pages 172

Ancient Law *by Henry Maine*   ISBN: *1-59462-128-4*   **$29.95**
The chief object of the following pages is to indicate some of the earliest ideas of mankind, as they are reflected in Ancient Law, and to point out the relation of those ideas to modern thought.   Religion/History Pages 452

Far-Away Stories *by William J. Locke*   ISBN: *1-59462-129-2*   **$19.45**
"Good wine needs no bush, but a collection of mixed vintages does. And this book is just such a collection. Some of the stories I do not want to remain buried for ever in the museum files of dead magazine-numbers an author's not unpardonable vanity..."   Fiction Pages 272

Life of David Crockett *by David Crockett*   ISBN: *1-59462-250-7*   **$27.45**
"Colonel David Crockett was one of the most remarkable men of the times in which he lived. Born in humble life, but gifted with a strong will, an indomitable courage, and unremitting perseverance...   Biographies/New Age Pages 424

Lip-Reading *by Edward Nitchie*   ISBN: *1-59462-206-X*   **$25.95**
Edward B. Nitchie, founder of the New York School for the Hard of Hearing, now the Nitchie School of Lip-Reading, Inc, wrote "LIP-READING Principles and Practice". The development and perfecting of this meritorious work on lip-reading was an undertaking...   How-to Pages 400

A Handbook of Suggestive Therapeutics, Applied Hypnotism, Psychic Science   ISBN: *1-59462-214-0*   **$24.95**
by Henry Munro   Health/New Age/Health/Self-help Pages 376

A Doll's House: and Two Other Plays *by Henrik Ibsen*   ISBN: *1-59462-112-8*   **$19.95**
Henrik Ibsen created this classic when in revolutionary 1848 Rome. Introducing some striking concepts in playwriting for the realist genre, this play has been studied the world over.   Fiction/Classics/Plays 308

The Light of Asia *by sir Edwin Arnold*   ISBN: *1-59462-204-3*   **$13.95**
In this poetic masterpiece, Edwin Arnold describes the life and teachings of Buddha. The man who was to become known as Buddha to the world was born as Prince Gautama of India but he rejected the worldly riches and abandoned the reigns of power when...   Religion/History/Biographies Pages 170

The Complete Works of Guy de Maupassant *by Guy de Maupassant*   ISBN: *1-59462-157-8*   **$16.95**
"For days and days, nights and nights, I had dreamed of that first kiss which was to consecrate our engagement, and I knew not on what spot I should put my lips..."   Fiction/Classics Pages 240

The Art of Cross-Examination *by Francis L. Wellman*   ISBN: *1-59462-309-0*   **$26.95**
Written by a renowned trial lawyer, Wellman imparts his experience and uses case studies to explain how to use psychology to extract desired information through questioning.   How-to/Science/Reference Pages 408

Answered or Unanswered? *by Louisa Vaughan*   ISBN: *1-59462-248-5*   **$10.95**
Miracles of Faith in China   Religion Pages 112

The Edinburgh Lectures on Mental Science (1909) *by Thomas*   ISBN: *1-59462-008-3*   **$11.95**
This book contains the substance of a course of lectures recently given by the writer in the Queen Street Hall, Edinburgh. Its purpose is to indicate the Natural Principles governing the relation between Mental Action and Material Conditions...   New Age/Psychology Pages 148

Ayesha *by H. Rider Haggard*   ISBN: *1-59462-301-5*   **$24.95**
Verily and indeed it is the unexpected that happens! Probably if there was one person upon the earth from whom the Editor of this, and of a certain previous history, did not expect to hear again...   Classics Pages 380

Ayala's Angel *by Anthony Trollope*   ISBN: *1-59462-352-X*   **$29.95**
The two girls were both pretty, but Lucy who was twenty-one who supposed to be simple and comparatively unattractive, whereas Ayala was credited, as her Bombwhat romantic name might show, with poetic charm and a taste for romance. Ayala when her father died was nineteen...   Fiction Pages 484

The American Commonwealth *by James Bryce*   ISBN: *1-59462-286-8*   **$34.45**
An interpretation of American democratic political theory. It examines political mechanics and society from the perspective of Scotsman James Bryce   Politics Pages 572

Stories of the Pilgrims *by Margaret P. Pumphrey*   ISBN: *1-59462-116-0*   **$17.95**
This book explores pilgrims religious oppression in England as well as their escape to Holland and eventual crossing to America on the Mayflower, and their early days in New England...   History Pages 268

www.**bookjungle**.com *email: sales@bookjungle.com fax: 630-214-0564 mail: Book Jungle PO Box 2226 Champaign, IL 61825*

QTY

The Fasting Cure *by Sinclair Upton*   ISBN: *1-59462-222-1*   **$13.95** ☐
In the Cosmopolitan Magazine for May, 1910, and in the Contemporary Review (London) for April, 1910, I published an article dealing with my experiences in fasting. I have written a great many magazine articles, but never one which attracted so much attention... New Age/Self Help/Health Pages 164

Hebrew Astrology *by Sepharial*   ISBN: *1-59462-308-2*   **$13.45** ☐
In these days of advanced thinking it is a matter of common observation that we have left many of the old landmarks behind and that we are now pressing forward to greater heights and to a wider horizon than that which represented the mind-content of our progenitors...   Astrology Pages 144

Thought Vibration or The Law of Attraction in the Thought World   ISBN: *1-59462-127-6*   **$12.95** ☐

by William Walker Atkinson   *Psychology/Religion Pages 144*

Optimism *by Helen Keller*   ISBN: *1-59462-108-X*   **$15.95** ☐
Helen Keller was blind, deaf, and mute since 19 months old, yet famously learned how to overcome these handicaps, communicate with the world, and spread her lectures promoting optimism. An inspiring read for everyone...   Biographies/Inspirational Pages 84

Sara Crewe *by Frances Burnett*   ISBN: *1-59462-360-0*   **$9.45** ☐
In the first place, Miss Minchin lived in London. Her home was a large, dull, tall one, in a large, dull square, where all the houses were alike, and all the sparrows were alike, and where all the door-knockers made the same heavy sound...   Childrens/Classic Pages 88

The Autobiography of Benjamin Franklin *by Benjamin Franklin*   ISBN: *1-59462-135-7*   **$24.95** ☐
The Autobiography of Benjamin Franklin has probably been more extensively read than any other American historical work, and no other book of its kind has had such ups and downs of fortune. Franklin lived for many years in England, where he was agent...   Biographies/History Pages 332

Name	
Email	
Telephone	
Address	
City, State ZIP	

☐ **Credit Card**   ☐ **Check / Money Order**

Credit Card Number	
Expiration Date	
Signature	

Please Mail to: Book Jungle
                    PO Box 2226
                    Champaign, IL 61825
or Fax to: 630-214-0564

ORDERING INFORMATION

web: *www.bookjungle.com*
email: *sales@bookjungle.com*
fax: *630-214-0564*
mail: *Book Jungle PO Box 2226 Champaign, IL 61825*
or PayPal *to sales@bookjungle.com*

Please contact us for bulk discounts

DIRECT-ORDER TERMS

**20% Discount if You Order
Two or More Books**
Free Domestic Shipping!
Accepted: Master Card, Visa,
Discover, American Express

www.ingramcontent.com/pod-product-compliance
Lightning Source LLC
Chambersburg PA
CBHW081158170626
46813CB00009B/3234